The Life of I

ON THE SĀDHANĀ TRAIL

Published by

Chinmaya Mission West
P.O. Box 129, Piercy, CA 95587 U.S.A.
Tel. (707) 247-3488
Email: publications@chinmayamission.org
Website: www.chinmayamission.org

First Edition: May 2016, 5,000 copies

Special thanks to Pūjya Guruji Swami Tejomayananda
for his loving support and guidance.

We gratefully acknowledge the team at Chinmaya Mission Los
Angeles for its study and notes on Pūjya Gurudev's works including:
Acharya Mahadevanji, Br. Vinod, P. P. Vaidyanathan, Kumar Singarju,
Viji Mahadevan, Pankaj Shukla, Nagaraj Pillutla, Rama Pillutla,
Susheel Mantha, Daya Gummi, Kshama Punj, Pavani Narayanadas,
Bala Bharadvaj, Priya Somasundaram, Priya S. Sharma; for pictures and
other resources: Suchit Nanda, Pranji Lodhia, and Bhaskar Chandan.
Our deepest gratitude to CCMT for every support.

Authors
Swami Ishwarananda and Nimmi Raghunathan

Editorial Support by the Mananam Team
Special thanks to Swami Shantananda
for his loving guidance to the Mananam team.

Margaret Dukes, David Dukes, Neena Dev,
Rudite Emir, Rashmi Mehrotra, Arun Mehrotra,
Padmashree Rao and Aarthi Ramalingam

Design & Layout
Preeti Chandan and Bluefish Designs team

Printed by
Silverpoint Press Pvt. Ltd., Mumbai, India

Library of Congress Control Number: 2016932118

ISBN: 978-1-60827-017-0

THE **mananam** SERIES
CHINMAYA BIRTH CENTENARY CELEBRATION SERIES

The Life of I

ON THE SĀDHANĀ TRAIL

CHINMAYA PUBLICATIONS
CHINMAYA MISSION WEST PUBLICATIONS DIVISION

Contents

Pujya Guruji with Pujya Gurudev

ॐ

Foreword

Excerpted from *Sādhanā-Sādhya-Viveka* by Guruji

What is *sādhanā*? The word *sādhanā* comes from the word *sādh*, which means to accomplish, or to achieve. To 'achieve' implies that there is something to be achieved and there is someone who wants to achieve. *Sādhan* refers to the means, the tools used to achieve the desired goal, and *sādhanā* means the practice. Also, the essence of *sādhanā* must be understood. Most people complain, "My life has become so busy that I do not have any time for spiritual practice." Such a complaint arises because of the erroneous idea that spiritual *sādhanā* is limited to a particular type of program, or actions, such as doing *pūjā* or *japa*. So, first we need to understand that *sādhanā* has two aspects. One is practice-oriented and the other is attitude-oriented. One approach is *kriyā-pradhān*; *kriyā* means action. The other approach is *bhāvana-pradhān*; *bhāvana* means attitude. Practice-orientation is when we make a daily schedule — to get up at a certain time, take a bath, sit down for some *pūjā*, *japa*, or scriptural study, and then meditate for some time.

That is a program or action plan for half an hour or longer. Such a program cannot be continued for twenty-four hours; it is not possible because we have to fulfill many responsibilities and perform other duties. So, the practice aspect of *sādhanā* will naturally be time-bound. However, we must practice this as well without fail. And, if one day we are not able to do the practices, then double the time the next day; for the mind is very cunning, and we must not yield to the mind's tendency to postpone or forget. This is time-bound, action-based discipline. The other aspect of *sādhanā* is attitude-oriented. Since attitude is not time-bound, it can make us full-time, permanent spiritual seekers. Gurudev used to say to those who attended his meditation classes that to have a very effective meditation in the morning for even ten or twenty minutes, the whole day and our entire life will have to be meditative, contemplative. And that is why, when somebody asked Gurudev, "How long should I meditate every day?" Gurudev replied, "Only twenty-four hours." That is possible only by a change in the form of vision directed by knowledge. The awareness that 'I am a spiritual seeker,' and understanding that every interaction and transaction with the world affects the mind, is the kind of awareness to be cultivated.

To illustrate, for someone who is allergic to certain ingredients in foods, there is an alertness to avoid those ingredients any time food is offered to them. Even little children who are allergic to nuts are so trained by their parents that if given a chocolate, they will ask, "Does it have nuts?" Similarly, a person must remain alert as a spiritual seeker and always keep the goal foremost in mind. The seeker needs to cultivate this understanding: "Whatever *sādhanā* I do will only be time-bound, but my attitude needs to be sustained throughout the entire day." Actions may change, but attitude should be constantly aligned to the desired objective. A devotee who follows *bhakti mārga* remembers that he is a devotee of the Lord, so whatever he does is for the Lord.

This is how we have to understand *sādhanā*: one is practice, which may change, and the other is attitude, which remains the same all the time. The attitude has to be constant. Even before sleeping, we can remember we have to wake up early for *sādhanā*. And, if situations entice the mind to stay up late, this trained attitude will help us to remain steadfast in our resolution. From another perspective, there are again two aspects of *sādhanā*, for achievement of any outcome — that which one has to do and that which must be allowed to happen. And this we must understand very well. To illustrate, to satiate hunger, cooking and eating the food is in our hands, but digesting happens automatically. Or for a gardener, preparing the soil, sowing the seed, watering the plant and all such actions are in his or her hands; but growth is not. The seed has to do that job. In *bhakti sādhanā*, to chant the name of the Lord is for us to do, but to give the vision of the form is in His hands. When the Lord wants to show His form, He will do so, but the chanting and praying are in our hands and we should continue to do so. What happens is that we do not do our part and yet worry that nothing special happened. So, in *sādhanā*, whether that *sādhanā* is of *jñāna mārga*, *bhakti mārga*, or *yoga mārga*, whichever the path —there is one part we must do —and another is to allow for the happening. Suppose there is a cut on the hand; we can apply medicine and bandage, but the wound has to heal from within itself. Continuing to open the bandage to check whether the cut has healed will not work; we have to allow it to happen. In the same way, the mind will be purified by *sādhanā*; and as long as the path is right, it will happen.

Two additional distinctions can be made in *sādhanā*. One is called preparatory *sādhanā*, and the other is the direct means. To gain Self-knowledge, the preparatory means purifies the mind. There are many methods given by the scriptures and teachers for such purification. *Satsaṅga*, pilgrimage, worship, *japa*, charity, and austerity are all various preparatory means to purify and concentrate the mind.

The direct means in one's *sādhanā* is to listen to Vedānta from the teacher — *śravaṇam*. After that, to reflect on what has been heard is called *mananam*. And then to meditate on it is *nididhyāsana*. That is the direct process of realization. So we should know the right means for the desired purpose. For the purpose of realizing the Self, we have to do *śravaṇam*, *mananam*, and *nididhyāsana*. To purify the mind — *yajña*, *dāna*, tapas, and the other methods are the means. So, one purpose or aspect of *sādhanā* is to purify the mind, and another purpose is to know the Self and abide in It. Just as the message in spiritual life is to look at spiritual life as a whole and live a whole life, there are some guidelines with respect to *sādhanā* also:

> First, let there be oneness in your vision. That means, to look upon all as one's own self.

> Second, let there be dedication in action. Perform an action and dedicate it to the Lord.

> Third, let there be equanimity of mind in accepting the results of action, or *asaṅgata*, non-attachment. Because when we have dedicated our actions to the Lord, there is no attachment.

To paraphrase in Hindi: *"drishti mein ektā, karma mein asangatā, aur karma phal mein samtā."* With the vision of oneness of the Self, perform all actions dedicated to God and accept all results of actions with equipoise. That is the central message of *sādhanā*, a great practice for all, at all times.

Tejomayananda

Swami Tejomayananda
Head, Chinmaya Mission Worldwide

Introduction

Imagine graduating *summa cum laude* and being told, as you get your college diploma, that your learning still lacks something. Not pleasant! But that's exactly what happened, the *Chāndogya Upaniṣad* tells us, when Shvetaketu returned home, swaggering a bit, after mastering the śāstras and the Vedas. Unimpressed, his father, the great sage Uddalaka, asked, "But do you know That one thing by which everything is known?" As Shvetaketu stood nonplussed, the sage said, "That can only be learned by those who inquire."

The world is full of the erudite and the bombastic. It is, after all, an age where individuality and independence are prized. This book, based on Pūjya Gurudev Swami Chinmayananda's bedazzling insight, wisdom, wit, and plain speaking, shows us how that powerful and ego-filled 'i' — the sure path to conflict and unhappiness — is to be discredited and redefined. The case for the banishment of 'i' is made, and tools are provided to accomplish this most challenging of undertakings. Then, all of us who have been prodded into inquiring may also hope, like Shvetaketu, to learn That by which everything is known. At the very least, we can hope to become better human beings than we are now, because there is no doubt that Gurudev's brilliance in thought and language will help us live a more wholesome life.

Interspersed throughout the text is the "Śrī Chinmaya Aṣṭottara Shata Nāmāvaliḥ," composed by Pūjya Guruji Swami Tejomayananda and Swami Shantananda. Each of the 108 names extolling Gurudev is also indicative of how the 'i' can be dispelled. An icon of a meditator is used as a metaphor next to each name to indicate the lesson each of it provides — to be reflected upon and put into action.

Finally, just as an enlightened Shvetaketu threw himself at the feet of his Master upon hearing the Mahāvākya "Tat Tvam Asi," we offer ourselves and this work at the feet of our Gurudev in gratitude and humility.

Cast of Characters

Anveshak: A skeptic in his late twenties, Anveshak likes nothing more than asking questions. He is uninformed about Hindu thought, but a good listener.

 **Dr. Sevadas**: Work, work, work — the three words that define him — he is praised by all for his tireless spirit and selflessness.

Shanti Sevadas: The doctor's wife is a picture of serenity. She engages body and mind in the worship of the Lord. For her, religion means Love.

 **Damayanti**: A yogini who every day seeks to push the physical body further. Being the best yoga practitioner in town, people line up to be her students.

Professor Vidyadhar: Widely read and very articulate, he has answers for Anveshak's never-ending questions.

 **Swamiji**: A monk at Chinmaya Mission, he delights in conversations with every true seeker and carefully guides them in their understanding of the philosophy of Vedānta.

Prologue : Tingling Awareness

What is happening in the world is not really the cause of our mental disturbances, but our relationship with them.

"I AM LOST!" he moaned.

Eyes red with tiredness and with legs buckling under him, Anveshak leaned on the car that he had just stepped out of and squinted at the bridge ahead.

It was not gold. And it was not a gate. Covered in fog, even from a short distance, the top of it was not visible. To Anveshak, the vision of the San Francisco Golden Gate Bridge seemed like a symbol of his own life: not golden, quite worthless and with a cloudy future.

Desperate and despondent, he dragged himself forward. Business debts were exploding around him, and losing his home to the bank was a very real possibility. No one that he had thought of as a friend, seemed like one now. Feeling like he had been kicked in the gut, Anveshak remembered again the harshness with which even his fiancée had dumped him. He was alone, so alone. Angrily, he yanked the ring she had given him from his finger and tossed it over the side of the bridge, watching its trajectory in the air and descent into the waters below. It was all over. There was nothing left. Everything seemed pointless.

Unshed tears in his eyes, Anveshak pulled closer to the edge of the bridge and peered down. The water below seemed tranquil, unlike his mind, and very welcoming. He wanted to forget everything and leave it all behind. The blue waters beckoned as his turbulent thoughts focused on his goal, cutting out all else. Quickly, he clambered over the railings and leaped onto the ledge below. Standing ramrod straight as the wind whipped around him, he let the memory of his dead mother wash over him. She had been so proud of him, and of his success. If he went to her now, she would know how to comfort him. With that thought, Anveshak was ready to step off the ledge, when he saw something appear in front of him. The apparition was gesturing to him to back off. He squeezed his eyes shut and opened them again quickly. The figure was still there, bearded and smiling faintly. Now a disembodied voice accompanied the visual: **"What you have is His gift to you. What you do with what you have is your gift to Him."**

What?!

The moment Anveshak tried to decipher what he thought he had heard, the noise of the real world around him penetrated his consciousness. Someone was crying out to him from the bridge above, and as he peered up he saw anxious faces looking down at him. Still slightly dazed from what he had seen and heard, he turned away from the edge of the ledge only to be immediately grabbed and pulled up. He was vaguely aware of a man urgently checking his eyes and pulse while asking him his name and age. He answered

ॐ गुरवे नमः Salutations to the teacher.

One can be a Guru only if one has the required magnanimity, the intimate personal experience of the Divine, and a great familiarity with the scriptures. In Him, we find all these and also unconditional compassion.

The Guru is not a person: He is the epitome of the spiritual goal. Walk steadily with him as the sole guiding light!

in broken syllables. A short time later, the man identified himself as a doctor and said that he was taking Anveshak to his office.

As he lay in the examination room, Anveshak let his eyes rove around. When they fell on the picture on the wall to his left, he froze. It was just as though the apparition had followed him and tucked itself neatly inside the frame! He sat up with a jerk, eyes wide in astonishment as he stared at the picture.

"My Guru!" came an affirmative voice from the doorway. Anveshak turned around to see the smiling doctor.

"I, I... saw, I have seen him," stammered Anveshak

"Really? You are a blessed man!"

"What is his name?"

"What? You said you had met him!"

"Seen him," said Anveshak impatiently. "Name, please?" he asked urgently.

The doctor turned toward the picture and replied with humility, "Pūjya Gurudev Swami Chinmayananda."

Anveshak could not speak, and overwhelmed with he knew not what, closed his eyes and thought, 'Did I really see him?' Was it just a coincidence that within an hour he was 'seeing' him again? Who was this? Hadn't he said something to him at the bridge? He forced himself to recollect — something about gift and... life.

Feeling a hand on his shoulder, he opened his eyes. Pointing toward the bottom of the picture frame, the doctor said, "Look, a special message for you!"

Anveshak read: **"What you have is His gift to you, and what you do with what you have is your gift to Him."**

Anveshak was astounded.

Karma Yoga

Purifying the Mind

The Signature of Life: Action and Interaction

Anveshak became a regular visitor at Dr. Sevadas's office. In the few weeks since he had hung on the precipice of life and death, Anveshak had stabilized emotionally to know that he would not repeat his desperate action again, no matter the provocation. But neither was he happy. He often asked himself, 'How is life a gift?' His limited reflection took him only up to the point of gratitude toward his parents who had given him the gift of life. Beyond that — what?

His new friend, the doctor, looking to help his dejected patient, one day casually asked him to come and help out at the office. Not sure what he could do, given that he had no particular expertise in the medical field, Anveshak resisted.

He had planned to get unemployment benefits and move into a small apartment. He was done. Work was overrated.

"No!" said the doctor. "It is not. Activity is what all of us engage in."

"Well, I don't want to."

Sevadas smiled and asked, "You have been through a lot recently. I am so glad you are alive. Aren't you?"

"Yes," answered Anveshak brusquely."I know that my life is a gift."

The doctor nodded, recognizing that Anveshak was being petulant, mouthing the words instead of fully believing that life was a gift. The doctor asked, "What are you doing with your gift?"

"Chilling," came the reply.

"Oh! You are engaged in some action then. Good," said Sevadas.

Anveshak stared back at him indicating the doctor had no idea what he was talking about.

Sevadas pointed out, "Even if you are just taking care of yourself by 'chilling' as you call it, you are acting."

When Anveshak continued to look stubbornly at him, the doctor was reminded of his own days when he had been cynical and impervious to the advice of his father. He remembered that singular day which had changed him forever. Sevadas had come home one evening to find a tall, ochre-clad man, full of cheer, seated in his parents' living room. Surrounded by a lively group of people, he was answering questions posed to him. The words he had heard Pūjya Gurudev Swami Chinmayananda utter that day still rang with crystal-clear clarity, 'Don't just do what you love; love whatever you do!'

The explanation that had followed the advice had been the most eloquent Sevadas had ever heard. Later, he had found many writings

---

ॐ लोकप्रसिद्धाय नमः Salutations to the one famous in the world.

A true Guru has an unmistakable aura, and the fame of a Guru who has transformed millions of lives is a tangible presence. Whenever he could, Gurudev used to visit a blind, 108-year-old saint. Once, Gurudev, with his wooden sandals on, walked across some wooden planks over a canal and reached the blind saint's dwelling place. When he entered unannounced, the saint correctly identified him and exclaimed, "Only one saint walks like that, and it is Chinmayananda. You walk like an army general!"

Any attempt to hide the self-resplendent sun will be futile. A true saint is like the sun; the world will know him even if he remains in solitude.

by Gurudev in his father's collection of books, and had devotedly read them over and over again.

Now he decided to explain what he meant by using the infallible words of his guru, Swami Chinmayananda:

> There is a fool, an idler. We ask him, "What are you doing, my boy?" He says, "Nothing." When he says, "Nothing," the answer does not mean that he is dead, but it means that he is not doing anything good with his activity, either for the society or for his family or for himself, because action must necessarily come out from him just as fragrance from the rose. The rose cannot stop its fragrance from spreading out. If it is a rose, it must have the fragrance of the rose. If it is water, there must be fluidity in it. It is its characteristic, it is its nature. Similarly, you and I, until we are placed in our burial ground, will have to act whether we like it or not.

"It is simple, Anveshak," the doctor continued. "My Gurudev used to say that life pulsating in the body is activity in the outer world. If we are alive, we have to act."

Anveshak immediately understood the logic of this. But he was still not sure he wanted to engage in any particular activity. The countless hours he had spent at work had led him to this pitiful state. All those tireless efforts later, he was still empty-handed. Of one thing he was sure: he definitely did not want to deal with failure again.

So he continued to argue, "And yet, if I did nothing, there would be no chance of failure, would there?"

ॐ ग्रन्थकृते नमः: Salutations to the author of books.

As the tongue of the temple bell strikes the bell cup, there is a harsh metallic sound. But as we listen to it, it warbles out a lingering melody before it slowly dies out into the very silence in which it was born. Similarly, the words of the scriptures have a harsh sound but a lingering ringing music. The harsh sounds are caught in a web of language and preserved in textbooks; but the warbling notes are to be produced in the secret cave of the seeker's heart.

Our first language is called our Mother tongue; we learn everything else through it. So also are the words uttered by the Guru — the scriptures reveal their secrets through his words.

Dr. Sevadas responded with Gurudev's words:

> The past can be used positively. But ordinarily we all get frightened
> and our own self-confidence goes away when we remember the
> past: In the past I was bad, so I can never be good. If the bad cannot
> become good, what is the meaning of good becoming good?

"That's a valid point," said Anveshak."Good cannot become good."

The doctor pushed further: "You know, Gurudev had also told us
that we get so embroiled in our past, we have no enthusiasm for the
present, and some of us are so anxious about how the future is going to
be, that again we forget to be in the present. Think about it. See where
you are in this spectrum of thoughts."

Eyes wide in surprise, Anveshak quickly realized the truth in this. Even
though he had not admitted it to himself, he was caught in the past and
terrified of the future. Somewhere in the deep recesses of his mind, he also
knew that if he did nothing and chose to remain just with his thoughts, he
might slip into depression. He needed to deviate from his current state.

"I do need a diversion," he murmured, "Maybe I should…" But
Anveshak had one more question before agreeing to working at the
office. "How do I know that I will do my job well? How do I know that
I won't make mistakes that will affect your work?" he asked.

"You already have the solution," beamed the doctor, "You want
diversion. You will have no time for self-pity or recrimination. Your

ॐ मनोहराय नमः Salutations to the enchanter of minds.

A guru enchants the hearts of every aspirant in a way quite indescribably
personal. Yet, the love and reverence a Guru evokes are also universally felt
by all disciples. The very nature of a Guru is both inclusive and unconditional,
and that expansive quality draws people from all walks of life.

Simplicity is the nature of all saints. A simple mind is always at ease with itself and with everyone else.

energies will be focused on the job at hand and what you need to do at a given moment. Keep your mind where your hands are working."

Was it as simple as that, Anveshak wondered.

The doctor pulled out Gurudev's *Kindle Life* from the bookshelf in his office and read out from the well-thumbed book:

Tiredness of life comes not because of physical exertion. Physical exertion cannot give you fatigue, you rest half an hour, and the physical body will revive itself. But the real fatigue is only the exhaustion of the mind, mental health can be maintained only when there is a greater goal in front of us to inspire us, and the higher the goal, the greater is the enthusiasm that inspires us. Having discovered a great goal, surrender yourself to that goal and act toward it, drawing your inspiration from that goal, and thereby discover a new column of energy. Do not allow this energy to be dissipated in the futile memories of the past regrets or failures, nor in the imagined sorrows of the future, nor in the excitement of the present. Thereby, the individual who is till now considered most inefficient finds his way to the highest achievement and success.

Anveshak took the book from the doctor's hands and began reading. Every page was a fount of inspiration, as though the book had been exclusively written for him. He just couldn't put it down.

Sādhanā

- Action is superior to non-action.
- Learn from your mistakes positively.
- Remain inspired.
- Live in the present.

To Give More Than We Take : Duty

"Gurudev said, '*The real joy is in activity where your head and heart can come together,*'" said Dr. Sevadas without looking up from the patient chart he was reading. It was past 8 P.M., yet the patients had not stopped coming. Anveshak was once again hovering around him, wishing the doctor would stop working and go home. "I am fine Anveshak, I am doing what I really want to do and it's also my duty to do this."

"Duty to whom?"Anveshak asked combatively. He wanted the doctor to take a break and, get some rest.

"In the context of spiritual growth, Gurudev has explained duty this way," said the doctor lifting his head to look at Anveshak. "*When you are enjoying the advantage of living in a community, you have obligatory duties to fulfill for the community.*"

"I don't see you enjoying anything," said Anveshak. "It's the community that keeps coming to you for help."

"They are not indebted to me, Anveshak! Let's not belittle anyone for whatever service they need, when we make use of other people's services all the time. Listen to what Gurudev said:

Take the roads for example. You and I enjoy driving on the roads. How many people have worked for making it available for us! Are you conscious of it? You write a check to buy a car. Are you grateful to the people who have worked for the construction of the car? When you are driving the car, are you grateful to them all? Just because you paid for the car and paid a road tax, your obligation is not over. We are not living independent lives, we live interdependent lives! We are living as indebted ones; we are not able to pay back even an iota of what we are enjoying for the hard work of a whole generation of people!

Anveshak felt uncomfortable hearing this. Although he had not cheated while he was running his business, paying his taxes on time, and following the legalities of running a corporation, it had nevertheless always been about making money and besting his peers at it. Should he have shown more support for the community? Was he not grateful enough? He continued to listen.

> Producers are few in every community in history — the ability to produce wealth is given only to a few. The majority in the community are consumers. So, why should I do it? You do it, and then you will understand — the joy that arises in you — that 'I am trying my level best to produce for the society.'

Anveshak resolved to keep this in mind. What was his duty? Was it predetermined? How should he know where his obligations lay?

ॐ कर्मपरायणाय नमः Salutations to the one always engaged in action.

The secret of all-enduring work lies in the depersonalization of the worker from his work. This is the secret of inspiration, and a work done under inspiration is certainly a thousand times more irresistible in its effectiveness.

Working with attachment leads to perspiration, not inspiration. Work should not exhaust oneself; it should only exhaust one's vāsanās.

"Yes, there is nitya karma, the daily duties that are incumbent upon you to be fulfilled every day, and naimittika karma, which are duties incumbent upon you on special occasions like a family wedding, and so on. These are your obligatory duties," the doctor explained.

"So all my duties were determined the moment I was born?"

Reflection: Swami Swaroopananda

Get yourself entirely involved in the study, devotion to Jagadīśvara, and daily abhyāsa. Don't 'look' left or right! There will be people and situations pleasant, not so pleasant, irritating, and even disturbing. Watch them all without getting upset, and discover each one expressing his own deeper vāsanās.

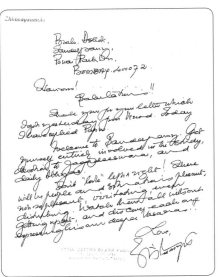

ॐ नारायणाय नमः **Salutations to Lord Nārāyaṇa.**

When a devotee asked Gurudev if he was not tired of working seventeen hours-a-day, his answer was: "If I were doing the work, I would have been exhausted, not just tired. But with Lord Nārāyaṇa Himself doing the work, why should I get tired?"

When work becomes worship, the worker will disappear and worship alone will remain.

"We don't live alone, so your duties are also determined by your environment. Gurudev has said that you have the power to change that environment. So, if you surround yourself with those who understand the community, nation, and the world better, your duties will reflect that."

After this, Anveshak did not raise a murmur about the long hours at the office. His work was not as exciting as the stock-broking business, which he had won and lost in, but neither was it stressful. Indeed, as the days went by, he came to enjoy the interaction with the people while manning the front desk. A smile, a kind word from him, or a helping hand to an elderly patient, elicited warm responses surprising Anveshak, who felt he was only doing his job.

He was doing it well!

Sādhanā

- Do your duty.
- Keep elevating the nobility of your duties.
- Never shirk responsibilities.
- Be a giver, not a taker.

Brood less, smile more, and serve all.

Dew Drops on a Lotus Leaf: Detachment

One day, ten-year-old Asha came in to see the doctor. Bright-eyed and chirpy, she stole the hearts of all. For the still healing Anveshak, she was a soothing balm, showing him the simple joys of life. They exchanged bits of candy, flowers, little drawings — till one day it all became too much to bear. He could not believe that the terminally ill child would leave them all soon. Furious, he charged at the doctor.

"Do SOMETHING. Get her well!"

"We are doing everything we can," came the steady reply.

"How can you say that? She is going to die!"

The doctor remained silent.

"I knew it. You don't care!" yelled Anveshak at the doctor. "You act like you can solve all problems, but you can't. You are a failure. All doctors are failures. The whole medical establishment is full of failures," he ranted.

The doctor still said nothing.

Weeks later, little Asha passed away. Dr. Sevadas continued

treating patients; there were many more like Asha he had to tend to. Anveshak was puzzled. How could the doctor not be affected by all the pain around him? How could he continue to carry on with his work?

"Joy and sorrow will be there in everything you do," the doctor explained."Didn't you know success in the morning when your stocks soared and then sorrow when they fell by evening? It was not that you had failed, but that the action did not materialize into the result you wanted."

"So act, act, act — but without care?"

"It's not a matter of not caring," the doctor clarified."Just learn to be detached."

"You mean be indifferent! It's the same thing!" cried Anveshak.

The doctor simply chose Gurudev's words to explain detachment:

> The shattering shocks in life are received by us only because we are making wrong contacts with the world around us. Our reaction to the environment will depend upon our mental evaluation of it and our inner nature at that particular moment. If our inward nature can be arranged, and continuously held in that arrangement, so as to make us react with the world positively, then we have discovered the secret of living in peace with the world, independent of all its happenings. This arrangement in one's inner nature is called detachment, and a personality that has developed detachment becomes a nonconductor of the shocks in life.

ॐ शान्ताय नमः Salutations to the peaceful one.

When he no longer identifies with the body, mind, and intellect, their conditions can no longer affect such a Man of Perfection. It is one of the surest symptoms of knowledge and saintliness if an individual is, under all provocative circumstances, infinitely at peace with himself and with the world.

Calmness and quietude belong to the mind; peace is the nature of the Self.

"I am not sure about this inner arrangement business." Anveshak was dismissive.

"There is a story Gurudev once told us. Tell me what you understand from it," said the doctor and paraphrased the story he had heard:

An old ascetic and a young ascetic were walking along a river bank when they saw a young woman drowning. The young monk jumped into the water, saved the woman, and carried her safely to the river bank. Then he continued to quietly walk behind the older monk.

Gurudev with Acharya Mahadevanji and his family

Reflection: Acharya Mahadevanji

Pūjya Gurudev was the one who pushed me into starting Bala Vihar in Southern California.

After he saw that things were moving along as he expected, he told me, "Let someone else do this job of coordination." At first I thought I had made some mistake, but after thinking about it, I found out that he was giving me a message. Never get attached to something, even if you enjoy doing it and are doing a good job.

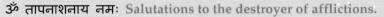

ॐ तापनाशनाय नमः **Salutations to the destroyer of afflictions.**

My reflection in the mirror depends upon the curvature of the reflecting surface. If it is concave, my reflection is short; if it is convex, it is long, and, if it is plain, it is my normal, natural shape and size. Similarly, happiness and sorrow do not belong to the Self. It is ever blissful. Sorrow and happiness belong to the 'reflection' — the ego alone!

The intensity of sorrow depends on the strength of attachment. Remove the mirror of attachment, and the reflection that brings sorrow can no longer exist!

After a while, the two sat down to rest under a tree when the older ascetic admonished the younger man that he had been wrong when he had carried the young woman. The young ascetic was surprised at the remark and responded, "Sir, I left her on the river bank, but you seem to be still carrying her!"

Reflection: Jorge-Luis Jauregui

Gurudev helped me see that action, when performed in the world with an attitude of karma yoga (without ego and egocentric desires), actually helps in purifying the mind so that it may abide more and more in the Knowledge of who I really am. So the family, the job, one's worldly duties, study of the scriptures, satsaṅga, independent reflection, contemplation, sevā, and serving one's Guru become spiritual sādhanā only when the sādhya (objective) is clear. Without viveka (discrimination between what is apparent and what is real), it is not possible to have

Jorge-Luis Jauregui with Gurudev

vāirāgyā (objectivity, dispassion), and without that, mumukṣutva (an intense desire to be free) can never be truly reached.

ॐ वीतरागाय नमः Salutations to the one free from attachment.

Three qualities that attach man to the world of objects are: a sense of reality of the objects, a belief in their permanency, and faith that they contain the potential for satisfying the craving for joy. He who, through the application of discrimination, understands that objects perceived through the senses are unreal, ephemeral, and do not contain an iota of joy — he alone is truly dispassionate.

Perceive through the senses, but do not allow the mind to get fascinated by mere perception.

Anveshak thought about it and said, "So you are saying that the young ascetic did his duty and unlike the older one, he was not bothered by the thought of who he helped or how he helped. He just responded to the situation."

"That, in other words, is detachment," said the doctor.

"What exactly am I attached to?" asked Anveshak.

"You! Yourself!" laughed the doctor."It is the feeling of 'I' and 'I want.' That's our problem. We have desires all the time. We are so attached to what we desire that we want each action to have the exact result we desired in the first place."

The doctor continued, "Gurudev told us to use our head. It is actually this capacity to think that separates the human from all other species, isn't it? He explained this so simply:

> You can live in this world as the mightiest of the mighty, a genius in the world — if adjusted properly, eliminating all disturbances. But we don't know how to. People live in this world like four-legged animals, prompted by the ego, instincts, impulses, without using the discriminative intellect.

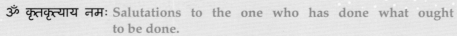

ॐ कृतकृत्याय नमः Salutations to the one who has done what ought to be done.

All that a seeker has to do to accomplish Godhood is to totally renounce his egocentric vanity and the satanic murmurings of his own impure mind of uncontrolled devilry! Detached from the false, attach yourself to the Truth! Therein lies the true redemption, and all successes and accomplishments.

To the accomplished, there is nothing to detach from. For, when the falsity is realized, can there be ownership?

"So you are saying when I get upset, I am not thinking? And here I am, believing that I was thinking too much about little Asha dying," said Anveshak.

"Ah! That's emotion, an attachment. Why didn't you feel as sad when another patient passed away? Why were you so upset when you lost money at the stock market, when you have seen others go down the same way before you?"

"Because I did not pause to think that there was no cure for Asha! With regard to my loss, I wanted to believe that I was not incompetent like the others, who lost while trading stocks," admitted Anveshak slowly.

"The answer you just gave points toward you 'thinking,' said the doctor. "Gurudev used to say, 'Life is a tragedy for those who feel. Life is a comedy for those who think!'"

A comedy? Anveshak was startled. After the roller coaster he had been on recently, he was ready for a laugh. Ruefully shaking his head, as he had not imagined he would ever be asking this, he posed his next question:

"Do you have pointers on how to think?"

Sevadas smiled.

Sādhanā

- Work enthusiastically without worry of result.
- Think and respond! Don't just react.
- Look beyond the 'I.'

IV

Intention Corrected: Desires

A couple of days later, when the staff was still working to complete the paperwork after the patients were gone, Anveshak approached Sevadas again. In fact, the doctor was expecting him.

Seated at his desk, and not even looking up from his computer, the doctor read:

> Every living organism on the surface of the globe is living this wondrous universal law of love, of tenderness, mercy, and kindness, except this half-intelligent, stupid man. And why? Because of his foolish ego and selfish desires.

He looked up to see if he had the young man's full attention and continued:

> Is not the tree giving out all that it has got? Is not every part of the tree in the service of mankind? Similarly, whether it is a bird or an animal, everyone, even the worms that are there — it is not consciously planned — but every one of these lives is serving the whole world. But for this environment, you and I will not be able to even exist. But man in his greed, in his selfishness, in his extreme desire to possess more and more, in his lust for things — he is the one who is stampeding the rhythm in the society.

"That was Swami Chinmayananda?" asked Anveshak as the doctor nodded and settled back in his chair. "Yes, it is he, the brilliant thinker!"

Anveshak paused. "Basically, I should not want?"

Reflection: Swamini Gangananda

Pūjya Gurudev told his students that a real seeker must practice the quality of nonpartiality, just as Guru and God are nonpartial. Thus, practice to be free from likes and dislikes. Practice nonviolence, and get rid of jealousy, hatred, and selfishness. But the real sādhanā is to reach the final goal — liberation.

"It is about changing what you want."

"You want me to become a tree? Or another Gandhi?"

"What's wrong with that? Being snide does not become you."

Anveshak looked mildly ashamed, as the doctor continued, "You wanted to know how to think. Take your lesson from nature. When you want something, it creates a thought, and that generates relevant action. So it is important to train yourself, your thoughts, to have the right kind of desires."

"And the right kind of desires are?"

"Selfless ones. Those that benefit the maximum number of people around you and replace the normal, selfish ones."

"So if I want everyone like Asha to be healthy in this world and I work toward it and I want it to happen very badly, am I being selfish?"

ॐ यज्ञकृते नमः **Salutations to the performer of yajña.**

Yajña is any social, communal, national, or personal activity into which the individual is ready to pour himself forth entirely in a spirit of service and dedication. Sharing the science of spirituality with earnest seekers, as well as the novice, is also yajña, for it is surely a noble service for the community to grow spirituality and live with love for each other.

Every act of sharing is a sacrifice. When it is done for the betterment of humanity, its status becomes equivalent to worship of God!

"Your action becomes more beautiful when the ideal you are working for is noble. You referred to Gandhi. Gurudev pointed out that Gandhi would probably have been a successful attorney if he had only worked to look after his wife and children. But when he sacrificed his life for everyone's freedom, he became a Mahātmā, a great soul! Wanting good health for all is not selfish. But tell me what happens if you fail? Will you go back to the Golden Gate Bridge?" asked the doctor.

Selfless suicide? Anveshak could not help but smile. The doctor was right. How can one be subject to suffering if the goal is unselfish?

"You told me that I should not be anxious about the results of my actions and instead I should just keep working. I think I have understood it. I will try and not get disappointed if I don't get what I want. I know it will be hard, but I have decided to give it a shot," Anveshak informed the doctor.

"Do remember that not worrying about the result does not mean you don't work or seek the best! Give it all you have. Gurudev said: 'Do the best; leave the rest,'" the doctor advised. After a pause he asked, "What happens if you begin to get results that make a difference to society?"

"I would have succeeded! I would have touched others' lives," exclaimed Anveshak.

ॐ ज्ञानमूर्तये नमः **Salutations to the one embodiment of Knowledge.**

A true painter never willingly sells his masterpiece! To him, that piece of canvas, upon which he has lavished long periods of effort, is by itself a complete reward, even if he be starving! If a mere piece of art could thus give invaluable joy to the artist, how much more intense must be the diviner joys of a perfect Saint, who is a personification of knowledge, working in the world of forms and names.

Every deed, word, and thought of a realized Saint is a masterpiece;
for all those are his offerings to the Almighty!

The doctor nodded as if expecting the answer and said, "You have understood that in your work you have to overcome selfish desires, but what you just displayed is called 'ego.'" Scrolling down on his computer, Sevadas read Gurudev's words:

Don't have the misconception that tomorrow onward 'I am going to be a great person.' NO. Even though you know it, tomorrow also you will be living as stupid a life as yesterday. You can advise others. But your life will be the same. It takes time and conscious effort, because each individual lives exactly as a prototype of his past.

Anveshak was taken aback.

The doctor continued with Gurudev's words:

Ego stands for the past. A bundle of past memories is called your ego. It is called 'me.' So, your stupid ego is only a bundle of memories of dead moments. Anything dead rots. Anything dead stinks. It is only when you look at the world through your stupid ego that it stinks.

Anveshak was chastised. He understood that his wanting to leap off the bridge a few months ago was driven by the monster called ego.

ॐ भारतगौरवाय नमः: Salutations to the pride of India.

Gurudev presented the scriptures directly to the public, unfolding their essence to all who would listen. He revealed the rich heritage of Sanātana Dharma, motivating Hindus to live as Hindus, to honor their own ancient culture, and to appreciate its relevance in today's world.

A true patriot puts the country or a noble cause above himself or herself. No sacrifice is authentic without such selflessness.

He had to eliminate desires that only pleased him, and he should not work driven by his ego — he got that.

But what was this past that Swami Chinmayananda and the doctor were going on about? His days at preschool? Elementary school, high school, college? What?

Sādhanā

- Observe nature, learn from its qualities.
- Drop your ego.
- Set higher goals.

Success or achievement is not the final goal. It is the spirit in which you act that puts the seal of beauty upon your life.

V

Becoming Footprint Free: Vāsanās

"You do know that you have had previous births, right?" asked Sevadas.

"I have heard about it," said Anveshak. "But I don't get it. First, you say, I have to live in the present. Now you are going on about how my past is affecting my present."

"Did you know my brother is a sculptor?" asked the doctor in a roundabout way.

"Nice!"

"We grew up in the same home and were raised by the same set of parents. He understands nothing about science and medicine, while I only see stone and metal where he sees beautiful forms. Do you know why this might be?"

Anveshak shrugged and kept looking at the doctor, hoping for an answer.

The doctor said, "Our great ṛṣis attributed it to our vāsanās."

"Which means?"

"Vāsanās are impressions of past actions leading to the tendencies in our present life; it is the end result of each and every action that we have engaged in with the idea of 'I am the doer' in our past lives."

"Like how a rubber stamp leaves an impression on paper?" asked Anveshak.

"Yes. A vāsanā is created when our Body, Mind, and Intellect encounter Objects, Emotions, and Thoughts. In every such contact, the end result is a 'tendency' created in you," the doctor explained.

"Good or bad tendency?"

"It depends on the action itself. Good acts lead to positive vāsanās and bad acts create negative vāsanās."

"How do vāsanās get expressed?" asked Anveshak.

"At the intellectual level as desires, through the mind as agitations, and as actions at the body level."

"And how do the vāsanās show up in me today?" wondered Anveshak.

"As your character," said the doctor. When Anveshak looked confused, the doctor said carefully, "Vāsanās create thought channels through which our mind flows, making us act in the same way over and over again. It leads to the formation of habits, which in turn shape our character."

"So, this is what is meant by the statement 'we are products of the past'? But don't we have any freedom from this?" Anveshak was astounded.

ॐ निर्विकल्पाय नमः **Salutations to the one free from wavering.**

In an aerial view of the world, there are no disquieting mental agitations, because in that vision of Oneness, little differences of opinion about a boundary line with a neighbor pale into insignificance. Similarly, when a spiritual aspirant raises himself into greater ambits of spiritual vision, his mind can no longer entertain any agitation at the ordinary levels of likes and dislikes.

Often detach yourself from the role you play, and look at the world with no reference to your body-mind-intellect.

"The vāsanās pressurize us to repeat ourselves. Gurudev said we are like parrots, repetitive. Every one of our actions is determined by our own inherent tendencies. This is because vāsanās influence the way we perceive, think, feel, and act; this cannot be easily overcome," the doctor said.

"But I don't want some past I know nothing about to control me now!" said a slightly agitated Anveshak.

"Our vāsanās get strengthened by repetitive actions prompted by them. In the process, we also create new vāsanās. We keep accumulating vāsanās life after life." The doctor sighed, aware that he had not broken free of this. "Doesn't your Gurudev have a solution for this?"

Reflection: Acharya Uma Jeyarasasingam

I met Pūjya Gurudev at a time when my mind was conflicted between leading a life of spiritual sādhanā and that of a householder. He straightened me out and showed me that there need be no conflict between the two and that a householder's life can indeed be well-suited for a life of sādhanā. Although I was a bit apprehensive as to whether I'd be able to do full justice to both, I nonetheless unreservedly resolved to do his bidding. Since then, there has been no conflict in my life.

ॐ उत्साहवर्धकाय नमः Salutations to the one who elicits enthusiasm in all.

To live in a routine will never yield the secret of living in inspiration. To get habituated to any method is to get into a rut and balk at all progress. Sādhanā is to be original at every moment — and to live ever in the white heat of inspiration, at once thrilling, divine, and ennobling.

Habits are unconscious repetitions. Practice is alert, vigilant, and conscious effort — new, every time!

"Yes, he does. The solution is to cleanse our mind and free it from the past."

"Cleanse? How? We are our past. You just said so! I don't think I can even wipe out stuff from last week and now you are saying we can do so from heaven knows when?" Anveshak's agitation was growing.

The doctor reached for the bookshelf again and found these words by Gurudev:

> The vāsanās are exhausted when you act on in the world without ego and egocentric desires. Then, existing vāsanās are exhausted and no new ones are created. So the pressure of vāsanās on the mind and intellect is reduced, and the mind's extrovertedness curtailed.

Smiling, Sevadas said, "You know, Gurudev never liked to eat eggplant, but he said that the more he tried to avoid eating it, the more it seemed to appear in front of him at mealtimes! This is to elucidate the point that our likes and dislikes are determined by our vāsanās. The trick is to not come under their spell."

"You mean Swami Chinmayananda should have enjoyed eating eggplant?"

"Not really. The lesson is that in the presence of the object or person of our dislike, we should train our mind to not entertain negative thoughts. This is the way to overcome our vāsanās."

ॐ निस्पृहाय नमः **Salutations to the one free from longing.**

When the true nature of a thing is not known, the human mind imagines things which are not there and the individualized ego sense arises, which becomes restless and discontented. The intellect plans various possibilities by which the confused ego can relieve its restlessness. These plans are called 'desires.' Therefore, the desireless state can be achieved only upon knowing the true nature of the thing.

Desires expressed through body are actions. Hence, actions can never bring an end to desires!

"Doing that is hard," said Anveshak, as images of those who had let him down in his business flashed in his mind.

"That is why I gave you the eggplant example. At first it's useful to attack the expression of the vāsanās at the physical level and not allow our sense organs to rule over our actions. Controlling the mind is a more gradual process."

Anveshak nodded as he began to understand the process of eliminating the influence of vāsanās.

Sādhanā

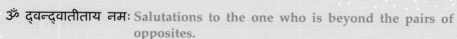

- Be alert against creating new habits.
- Exercise your freedom of choice.

ॐ द्वन्द्वातीताय नमः Salutations to the one who is beyond the pairs of opposites.

Likes and dislikes, success and failure, joy and sorrow, and such other pairs-of-opposites are the wheels on which the mind rolls forward, earning experiences in life. To free oneself from the pairs of opposites is to be free from all the limitations of mortal existence among finite objects.

Your eyes can see both light and darkness, and your ears can listen to both sound and silence. If so, what is their natural state? Emulate that neutral state in your mind.

VI

Attitude, Attitude, Attitude

Anveshak was gradually feeling healthier, both inside and out. He came in regularly to the office, made friends with the rest of the staff and was an efficient and ideal employee. Emotionally he felt stable and no longer evinced interest in the charged world he had engaged with earlier. His favorite hour of the day now was when he got to spend time talking to Sevadas after everyone had left the office.

The doctor, keeping in mind Anveshak's fragile emotional state, had at first indulged him, but soon found him not only an eager learner but also one who practiced what he had understood. Even better, he came back to vocalize his experiences and thoughts, engaging in a dialog that Sevadas had come to delight in.

One day, as he stood observing the front desk, he saw the young man smiling and speaking with a patient who was also animatedly responding to him. And yet, Sevadas sensed restlessness in Anveshak. He knew Anveshak would hang back that day, after work, to talk to him.

ead **Ask** Discus

Learn Do

🖋 Join the discussion on
Sadhana for self-discovery.

🖋 Interact with characters
in the book.

🖋 Chat with authors.

DO NOT MISPLACE
this bookmark
until you register at
www.sadhanatrail.com

Your log in id: Password
LOI-01464   A423HHh

here is no achievement more so
glorious than the realization o
identity with the unlimited, ete
                    -Swami Chinma

Come.
Hold His Hand.
Walk With The Master.
Discover Your Self.

Sure enough, questions flew at him in the evening. "All this business of fighting off the vāsanās is not working. What am I not doing right?"

"Why do you think it is not working?" asked the doctor.

"The past is very difficult to give up. The young patient who came in today, while he waited to see you, started talking to me about the stock market and the shares he had invested in, and I was more than ready to engage with him about it," explained Anveshak.

"You gave him your expert advice?"

"Yes, but it comes to me now, that I had slipped back to my past without even realizing it."

"There is nothing wrong with that, Anveshak," said the doctor. "Pūjya Gurudev continued to write even after he took to monastic life. He began his life writing as a journalist and socialist, and sustained that brilliant talent later as a monk and spiritualist."

"So his vāsanās continued?" asked Anveshak.

ॐ जीवन्मुक्ताय नमः Salutations to the one liberated while living.

A perfect sage cuts himself free from all attachments; with a mind well-balanced under the light of his own wisdom, he has been completely liberated from the chains of all moral debilities, ethical imperfections, and sensuous appetites.

Freedom from the mind is true freedom; one does not need to live in seclusion to achieve this.

Reflection: Acharya Shailaja Nadkarni

When we were about to buy a small house for Chinmaya Mission in Orlando, Florida, I showed Pūjya Gurudev the photo of the property and asked for his blessings. He asked me, "Why all this?" Then he called me and said in my ear, "Do everything, but remember that you are doing nothing."

"Yes, but his attitude changed!"

Without asking any details, the doctor said, "Change your attitude toward work, and also while working, Anveshak."

"Okay, by doing what?"

"Finding God in your work," said the doctor quietly, knowing that Anveshak was not a believer.

Anveshak stared mulishly at the doctor. Up until now, there had been so much clarity and rationale in their discussions, but now this?

When he said nothing, the doctor plowed on, "The temptation is to condemn God for one's troubles and failures. But in order to work with enthusiasm and dynamism, everyone needs an altar. It doesn't have to be God, it can be the altar of your professional ambition, an ideology, or an object of love. You obviously love the unpredictability and challenges of the stock market, so there is nothing wrong in

ॐ पावकाय नमः *Salutations to the purifier.*

The practice of attaching our attention to the Higher and thereby detaching from the lower is the 'inner purity' which is possible only when the Guru effectively creates the curiosity to live as the higher Self in the mind of a seeker. Such trained minds become fit for plunging into the study of scriptures.

Fire is the great purifier which burns all blemishes; Guru is like a fire, and a seeker should allow him to burn all of one's sinful thoughts.

advising people just as you did with the young man. We all work for someone or something we love. The thing is, it is the altar of God alone which offers an unparalleled steadiness that nothing else can."

Anveshak was still silent, but the doctor saw that he was listening.

"Do you know what you have to offer at the altar of God, Anveshak? Not your money, nor your friends, but the results of all your actions, your ego. Since you have many desires and mental agitations, I am telling you this. If you can get your thoughts on God, you will find that your mind is effortlessly controlled. The nature of your desires will change. Your vāsanās will change."

Anveshak was still not convinced.

"You wanted to be free. What happened?" asked the doctor, in a bid to make him talk.

"I do! Instead of telling me how to rid myself of vāsanās, you keep talking about something else," Anveshak argued.

"Vāsanās are not the enemy. Your identification with the vāsanās and their expressions are the problem. Change your thought process, attach yourself to God; you will be free."

"Are you?" he asked the doctor.

"Am I what? Attached to God? Not enough," admitted the doctor, who believed so strongly in the path of service, worked long hours, treated everyone equally, but was still not able to surrender his thoughts to the Lord.

ॐ क्षमाशीलाय नमः Salutations to the one of forgiving nature.

The capacity of the mind to accommodate cheerfully all its vicissitudes and patiently ignore any obstacles that might come its way is true endurance. In the inner revolution of an individual to free oneself from psychological and intellectual confines, endurance ensures success.

To react and retaliate is weakness; to endure is strength. Patience fosters and fortifies peace!

"Is that why you get annoyed so often?" asked Anveshak curiously.

The doctor sounded rueful, "Yes. But I can show you what it means to surrender to the love of God."

"Meaning?"

"Will you come home with me this evening? I would like you to meet someone."

Sādhanā

- Work with an attitude of surrender.
- Dedicate all to the Higher.

ॐ ज्ञानतृप्ताय नमः **Salutations to one reveling in Knowledge.**

The reflection of the sun in a cup of water can be broken up when the water in the cup is shaken. But when the water is poured out, the reflection ends, and no more can the sun in the sky be shaken by any known method. The sense of discontentment belongs to the misconceived notions of the ego-center. Ego is the reflection of the Self that is contained in the cup of intellect, and when the ego is destroyed by Knowledge, the Self-realized one will shine like the sun in the sky.

Ego and the Self are two sides of the same coin; if you identify with the ego, you fail to abide in the Self.

Bhakti Yoga

Filling the Heart

VII

Understanding Love: Silence and Surrender

The sweet smell of jasmine and 'something else' that Anveshak couldn't immediately identify wafted through the air as he stepped into the foyer of Sevadas's home.

For the doctor it had been a long day at work that had included obstinate patients. Anveshak knew the doctor was holding on to the last tethers of his patience when the latter had to attend to a demanding patient just as they were preparing to close at the end of the workday. So Anveshak had been quite ready to head back to his apartment instead of accepting the tired doctor's invitation to visit his home. But Sevadas had not forgotten, and he urged Anveshak to come along and meet his wife Shanti.

Now here he was, enveloped by floral scents as he crossed the warm and welcoming foyer into a living room that was filled with indoor plants and paintings of temples. Fully attuned to what he was viewing, he was jolted back from his musings by the intrusive ring of Sevadas's phone. As the doctor stepped out to take the call, Anveshak had a sudden insight. The 'something else' that had floated toward him as he entered the home was — silence!

It was not the oppressive kind in which fear drives out voices. And it certainly was not the kind of dark silence that had just recently taken him to the Golden Gate Bridge. This was an undemanding, serene kind of silence; it had a certain depth that made him relax effortlessly. Anveshak couldn't grasp how he knew the difference. All that he knew was what he felt: comfortable and quiet.

As he sat there examining his feelings, he heard a sound. It was again a ringing, but this time, he heard bells accompanied by soft singing. Unbidden, his feet carried him toward the voice. He stood at the doorway of a room, mesmerized by what he saw. A huge picture of Gurudev Swami Chinmayananda graced the wall facing him. A smile played on Gurudev's lips, and he seemed to be glancing at Anveshak, almost beckoning him into the room.

A small movement caused him to be distracted and broke the trance he was in. He looked at the lady who was seated on the ground in front of the picture and the altar that had deities adorned with jasmine flowers. He lowered himself to the ground to sit beside her and watched as she finished singing and conclude her pūjā, of which he frankly understood very little.

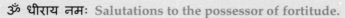

Having completed the pūjā, she glanced at him, and offered a whole fruit from the bowl by the altar. One look at the gently smiling lady and it at once had him bowing his head and taking the offering from

---

ॐ धीराय नमः **Salutations to the possessor of fortitude.**

Equanimity should not flow from the dark caves of one's stupidity and inertia, but it must gurgle forth from the open sunny fields of wisdom and understanding. When one understands the essential nature of the objects to be finite, out of that realized knowledge, such a wise one gains enough balance from calm endurance and does not feel exalted in pleasure or dejected in pain.

When you watch a game without taking sides, you enjoy the game.
So also is the vision of the wise about life.

her. Anveshak noticed how she was unperturbed by his presence. Had she been informed by the doctor?

Serene. That was the word that came to mind as he looked at her. After a round of introductions, when he learned she was the doctor's wife and that her name was Shanti — which he thought was delightfully apt —he could not restrain himself from rushing in and asking her about her serene demeanor and the tranquility that permeated the home.

Laughing, she said with a soft smile, "I am in love! And our home is filled with it!"

Anveshak almost blushed at this declaration from someone older than him. "The doctor is a good man..." he began, but was interrupted by a gently chuckling Shanti.

"Yes, he is! But I am in love with Kṛṣṇa."

Anveshak couldn't believe his ears. Who was that? Wasn't Dr. Sevadas's first name Anmol? "Krrr..ishna?" he stammered.

But Shanti continued with great tenderness, "Rāma... Śiva... Bālāji..."

Anveshak had had enough. "Please. Please stop," he said a little strongly. "Shantiji, I owe my life to your husband and I don't want to hear more!"

He was greeted with tinkling laughter.

Shanti pointed to the altar. In a voice filled with mirth, she said, "Here are those who help me betray your dear doctor."

Anveshak smacked himself mentally. His thoughts had been so far from the altar and the Gods that he had not picked up on the obvious. "And your husband...?" he began hesitantly.

"There is love there, too, Anveshak," Shanti said softly, "but it's different."

He knew that. "Of course, Shantiji, after all, these are all just lifeless idols."

"They are not just idols. Each of them represents qualities that I admire and want to emulate," explained Shanti. "I want the compassion of Lord Śiva, the nobility of Rāma, the playful maturity of Kṛṣṇa."

Anveshak just stared at her. Then waving his hand toward the altar he said, "So, you do all this to gain all that?" And how exactly does an idol pass those qualities on to you?"

Shanti pointed to the mangalsūtra around her neck. "This chain is not my husband. It is a symbol representing our commitment to the marriage. It's a reminder of our bond, who he is, and who we are together. It's the same symbolism with what you say are mere idols. They represent lofty ideals!" Observing that Anveshak was not completely convinced and impulsively wanting him to be, she decided to take recourse to the words of Gurudev to reinforce what she had said. "I am sure my husband has talked to you about Gurudev. About worshiping God, Gurudev said:"

> Why do you keep your wife's picture and children's picture on your desk? So that you may always remember them. Similarly, in the practice of devotion a form is necessary for the mind to lift itself.

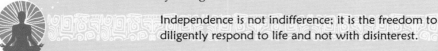

ॐ निरपेक्षाय नमः Salutations to the one free from expectation.

One who draws inspiration, fulfillment, and joy from deep within himself is independent of the world outside. He does not bind himself to the vicissitudes of worldly life and therefore keeps his mind above the storms of uncertainties that situations may bring.

Independence is not indifference; it is the freedom to diligently respond to life and not with disinterest.

And when the mind is seeing the form, you are not worshiping the form — you are worshiping what the form stands for. Every idol stands for an ideal.

"What he said felt so true; I have never forgotten it," Shanti told a now slightly pliant Anveshak.

But she raised his hackles almost immediately: "I want to lose myself in that idol," she said in a low tone, but with an unmistakable fervency.

"A God in metal and stone!"

Reflection: Swami Prakashananda

It was 1992. We were having the suvarṇatulābhāram for Gurudev in Sidhbari. Standing in what seemed to be an unending line, we were all doing parikramā of Gurudev. My eyes were fixed unflinchingly on him. I approached eagerly, desiring his compassionate glance. When I was about one-and-a-half meters away from him, he lifted his eyes to mine and put his hands together, giving the sweetest and most humble namaskāra that anyone has ever done. I was blown away. That day, I understood what humility was. Here was the world's foremost authority on the *Bhagavad-gītā*, a living example of a Ṛṣi, the very embodiment of all the teachings of the Upaniṣads, offering namaskāra, with folded hands, to one so lowly and insignificant. Only Bhagavan can do it!

ॐ समबुद्धये नमः Salutations to the one with an even mind.

Surrender of the ego is the unveiling of the Divine in oneself, and the degree to which the Divine is manifest, to that degree the individual raises himself in his potency to face life and to remain equanimous in all circumstances.

Divinity is everyone's true identity. When we discover this, we find equanimity under all conditions, at all times!

Shanti closed her eyes and said, "To lose oneself means to become dear to Him." In the ensuing silence, she said from memory:

> The Lord says, One who is equal toward friends and foes, one who is equipoised, balanced, and same in honor and dishonor, one who is equal in joys and sorrows arising out of heat and cold — such a one is dear to Me. (*Bhagavad-gītā*, XII.18)

Shanti opened her eyes. "That's what Lord Kṛṣṇa has said in the *Gītā*. And Gurudev said it might seem as though the Lord loves a devotee who behaves like a stone, or a statue, and is unfeeling. But if we ignore the discomforts that our body faces at the physical level, the churning emotions of our mind, and the subjective understanding of our intellect, what we are left with is pure love."

Anveshak couldn't stop himself from voicing his irritation: "Feeling nothing somehow amounts to love? Isn't love all about feeling? At least your husband is not indifferent like you. He goes out and helps people in pain."

"I admire my husband like none other, Anveshak. His service to all is an expression of his love. If he didn't care deeply for others, he could not go out and do what he does, day after day," Shanti spoke with kindness despite Anveshak's outburst. "But have you seen how tired he is by the time he gets home? At work he is easily agitated. I am sure you have noticed."

ॐ फलासक्तिरहिताय नमः Salutations to the one free from attachment for results.

If one can work surrendering one's ego and egocentric desires to enjoy the fruits of one's labor, one can thereby achieve a sense of fulfillment and a great peace arising out of the exhaustion of the vāsanās. Reducing the influence of one's own vāsanās is the way to true freedom!

One cannot comprehend the influence of vāsanās until one observes oneself carefully in the field of action. Both attraction and repulsion are caused by vāsanās.

She continued, "I am going to explain this to you with something Gurudev has said." Anveshak nodded and she quoted again from memory:

> When people say they are exhausted, it is all a mental dissipation. The values we maintain in our intellect determine the quality of our thoughts, the type of our relationship with the world outside. If these values are wrong — if the thoughts, the relations with the world are wrong — then unnecessarily you have to waste a lot of mental energy in meeting a simple challenge outside.

Anveshak did not understand. Was she saying that the values that her husband lived by were wrong? How could helping people get well be wrong even if it meant exhausting oneself?

Shanti looked at him and continued:

> We must give up our unintelligent wish for a life of fulfilment with the props of things from outside ourselves and with the patronage of other beings around. Our love is poisoned by the spirit of gratification which we expect to gain through what we do.

Anveshak shrugged, "Then how should one help others?"

Shanti replied simply, "Stop playing God." When Anveshak quirked an eyebrow at her, Shanti smiled and used Gurudev's words again:

> Serve the world, yes. Each individual is given a certain field where he can serve. But don't try to take the responsibility of God. Certain things God alone can do — yield unto Him.

ॐ विनोदप्रियाय नमः Salutations to the one who loves humor.

One who has realized the Absolute is forever free and light-hearted. Once, a woman came to Gurudev and said, "Gurudev, I want peace." Gurudev was always quick-witted and jovial. He told her, "Oh, why did you not ask me earlier? I left that bottle of peace syrup on my table. I could have brought it for you and given you a few drops."

Humor lightens the heart, invigorates the spirit, opens the mind, and invites others to be near you! Laugh!

Recalling an earlier conversation with the doctor, when the latter had confessed he was unable to dedicate himself to God as much as his wife did, Anveshak asked, "How do we know what we should do and what God is supposed to do? Doesn't it lead to indifference?"

"In every situation do your best, but without any anxiety about what it turns out to be. Indifference is not a passive attitude if you understand it correctly, Anveshak. Hindu scriptures use the Sanskrit word udāsīna, which means participating without prejudice," said Shanti, and then recollected what Gurudev had said on the subject:

> Should you neglect your old father and mother, and help poor people in another country? Your own brother is rotting in the streets, and should you build shelter for the homeless? Start from home and serve all. Do what you should and what you can. The rest you just surrender to the Lord. This is called indifference. This does not mean that you are not affected by anything. Do the best and leave the rest. Surrender the rest to the Lord and His infinite justice, and forget all about it. Learn to be indifferent to things you have no control of. Or else, your mind has no time or energy.

Shanti continued, "Surrender is a silent submission to the will of God."

Anveshak wondered. Was surrender in silence? Or did surrender lead to silence?

Sādhanā

- Function effectively within your realm of activity.
- Remain untouched by bodily discomforts.
- Be indifferent to the sway of emotions in the world outside.
- Make your intellect a storehouse of right values.
- Acceptance leads to equipoise in any situation.

VIII

Rising in Love: Freedom

Anveshak was intrigued. Every conversation he had recently had seemed to end with the idea of surrender. So now he wanted to know: What exactly was going to happen if he 'surrendered.'

"Freedom will be yours," replied Shanti.

"By giving myself up to something I don't understand or can't see, I become free?" a slightly incredulous Anveshak asked.

"Well, the first step is to know true love," said Shanti, and looked up to see Anveshak flinching. He had a fleeting glimpse of it, but his business downturn had led to his fiancée abandoning him. Shanti's face showed compassion as she felt the pain of all the loss that he had faced in his young life. Seeking to soothe, she placed her hand on Anveshak's arm and suggested that they have dinner first and then continue their discussion.

The meal was a simple one, albeit a pleasant one, with both Shanti and Dr. Sevadas chatting about their day and encouraging each other. To Anveshak their interaction was interesting to observe, and very different from his experience when he had known love.

While he helped the couple clear the table and do the dishes after dinner, he spoke forthrightly of what he had just witnessed. Shanti glanced at her husband, and when he acquiesced, she said, "You know how we were talking earlier of dissipation of energy? Gurudev has more to say on it."

Please don't bind another with your love. Because you make the other fellow also dissipate energy along with you. Then what should be my relation with others? Toward all around you, just be friendly. In friendship, I love you, but you are not tied to my will. You have every freedom to do what you like. Lovers always want to force the beloved to do whatever they want. That is the quality of a possessive lover. If it is friendship, each has all the freedom to do what he likes. You still love like a friend. There is no bondage. It is pure love.

Not sure he understood this at all, Anveshak stood silently by the kitchen sink looking from wife to husband and back again. Everything he knew about love seemed to have been turned upside down.

"Were you in love, Anveshak?" asked Shanti. Not meeting her eyes, he barely nodded his head.

"When I asked you that question, what did it mean to you?" she probed.

"Whether I had a girlfriend."

Shanti nodded, as she handed some dishes to her husband to put away. "That's what we all think love is. That it is a moment in time when we have fallen in love with another. But, as you yourself have experienced, it is not permanent and we come to feel the misery of being alone when separated from the other. Am I right?"

Anveshak gestured in agreement. He was not going to easily forget the agonizing pain of losing the fiancée he had loved so intensely.

He pulled himself back to the present as he heard a beaming

ॐ मधुरस्वभावाय नमः Salutations to the one of sweet nature.
Every gesture of a great guru bears the mark of tender thoughtfulness. Once, when a devotee who was serving Gurudev had completed her task and was about to leave his room without turning her back toward him, he said to her: "Please turn around. I can't close the door in your face."

Love has no language. But, love is the language of the Divine!

Sevadas say, "That's because, as Gurudev said, we really don't know *how* to love. Instead of rising in love, we always *fall* in love!"

Shanti added, "The mistakes we make are because of our rush to forget our sense of what Gurudev called 'separateness.' He has pointed out that what we term as disobedience of a child, is actually the first act of asserting one's individuality to break away from the possessive love of the mother. But that is also when we begin to feel alone. And from then on, we keep working to overcome that separateness."

"We want to be loved," Anveshak understood correctly.

Shanti responded with Gurudev's words:

Since we have misunderstood that 'being loved' is love, we always try to be good, cheerful, smart, to dress-up well and to appear beautiful, so all may love us. The individuality in each of us, in its loneliness, seeks its escape in a thousand ways — and they have all come to be accepted in our society.

She continued, "That's why we have marriage celebrations and all kinds of other functions. We want to escape our separateness so much

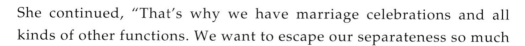

ॐ सुहृदे नमः Salutations to the friend of all.

To cultivate a broad-minded attitude that befriends the whole world, the Guru says, "Silently hear everyone. Accept what is good; reject and forget to remember what is bad. Accept all and take only what you need; reject the rest and live happily."

Freedom cannot be enforced; it can only be reinforced as one's own birthright through friendly advice!

that we rush to belong to a person, group, state, or country. This kind of love is always for mutual benefit. There is togetherness, but for it to continue, both parties are required to enrich the life of the other. There is fear of loss in it. It can be broken at will, Anveshak. And, if and when the other side stops giving love, you stop, too, don't you?"

Anveshak did not want to think any more about his past, and the painful deprivation he felt. Shantiji was right, it had all been transactional.

Noting that she had Anveshak's full attention, Shanti said, "That is a lower kind of love."

This gentle lady in front of him was full of surprises. "Which means there is something like a higher love?"

"Yes is the short answer," said Shanti. "I can give you the long answer if you want," she offered and Anveshak was quick to assent.

"Higher or lower, it is the same emotion. Both are born of a person identifying with another. The intensity of love is decided by the intensity of identification. But it is the object to which love is directed that makes a difference. When it is directed toward those mentioned already, it is sneha, or lower love. But when we direct our emotions to a more inspiring ideal, God, it is premā. When we offer that love to God with no expectation in return, it is bhakti, or devotion, the highest possible form of love," she explained.

ॐ जनप्रियाय नमः Salutations to the beloved of the people.

A spiritual seeker has a healthy attitude toward things, and he keeps a balanced relationship with everything around him in life. He loves all and fulfills his duties toward them. But he never allows the world of relationships around to bind him and loot him of his freedom to grow.

The difference between love and attachment is this: loving all is love, loving only a chosen few is attachment!

She thought for a short moment and then quoted Gurudev:

> Sacrifice is the price you pay for devotion. Devotion in our heart, when it pervades through our relationships in the world outside becomes true bhajana. Thus, if love (bhakti) is the emotion, service (bhajana) is its expression.

Sevadas slipped out of the kitchen — he had calls to return, patient files to review. He knew what his wife would say: That service and love were inextricably linked and he needed to go into the pūjā room more often. Shanti observed his exit and sighed. She wondered when she would be able to get him to turn his love toward God and surrender to Him.

Reflection: Swami Abhedananda

In the early 1980s when I was ten years old, I had won a competition for writing the most number of names of the Lord. Pūjya Gurudev asked me, "Who helped you? Your mother, father, grandfather?" I shook my head saying, "No." Gurudev took my hand and said, "I know who helped you, it is God." And while saying these words, he took me in his arms and embraced me tightly. It is the same embrace that I can permanently feel in myself today and now. It was a silent initiation, during which he took my heart into his heart and gifted Himself to me forever.

ॐ भयनाशनाय नमः **Salutations to the destroyer of fear.**

One who is free from desires has no more attachments with any particular objects of the world, and, naturally, there cannot be any sense of fear. He has, in his true wisdom, realized the shadow-nothingness of his dream-body, and so does not fear even death, which to him is only an escape from his own self-created body cocoon!

Fear presupposes attachment. It also indicates that we are foolishly trying to deny the inevitable mortality of matter!

But for now she turned her attention to Anveshak, who stood rooted in his spot, wanting to hear more.

"In this love, we don't have any expectations. We don't ask, we don't beg. We just give and give. We become creditors, not debtors. We become wealthier than all of Wall Street. Haven't you noticed how getting a gift could be exciting, but giving one is so much more satisfying? In the same way, love grows by giving more and more love. There is so much happiness in giving love at the divine altar that there is no loneliness and sense of separateness. That love is ours and is ever present. Experiencing that, we become completely free from dependence on others," said Shanti, adding "It is freeing. That's why Gurudev said we did not have to 'fall' in love, rather 'rise' in it."

Freedom was something Anveshak really, really wanted. He had been through too much and had realized the impermanency of friendship and money. He was willing to experiment with what Shantiji was claiming to be a hard fact.

"How do I rise in love with God?" he asked.

Sādhanā

- Seek to be free of dependence.
- Cultivate relationships that allow free thought and action.
- Be like your mother, give and give more love without expectation.

At all times, send out love to all, kindness to all, blessings to all. Soon you will find all, including your enemies showering you with love.

IX

Being in Love: Never Being Alone

"Remember the Kargil War?" Shanti asked Anveshak as she ushered him back to the pūjā room. "Soldiers had to defend the boundaries of India. They suffered, their families suffered, they functioned under the direst of conditions. But you know what kept them going? Love for their country. It is only where love is present that work can be so wholehearted."

"Like our doctor, Shantiji?"

"Yes, his service is love in action. But do you understand what quality underlies his work and the actions of the soldiers?" Shanti asked, sitting down.

"Anxiety for the well-being of what they love?"

"Yes, Anveshak!" Shanti was pleased. "If love is sincere, it is accompanied by great sensitivity. When we love someone or something truly, we want them to be happy and in a good state at all times. We anticipate their needs and their feelings, even before they are expressed, and work to satisfy them. Our ego is put aside while we are focusing on the object of our love."

"My mother was that way," said Anveshak with a distant look.

Shanti sat quietly, giving him the time to reminisce. Then she asked softly, "You obviously loved her. Did you respect her, too?"

Anveshak nodded, his heart full. Shanti saw the full play of emotions on his face.

"She loved and respected you, too, I am sure," she said.

Gathering himself together, he looked up at her questioningly. Shanti responded to his silent query, "Well, it's obvious from the memories you seem to have of her. When someone loves and respects another, Gurudev said, he or she experiences reverence. It allows the other person to just be."

"It is always tempting to try to change people into what we want them to be," added Anveshak. "My mother obviously knew what you are talking about to me today, because she accepted me for who I was and allowed me to grow and become what I am now. As long as she was there, I had her full support even when I made mistakes. But I don't have that now." He choked back his tears. He had felt her absence most keenly just before he had made that fateful walk to the edge of the bridge.

"Anveshak, the things we have talked about just now — sincerity, sensitivity, reverence, understanding — offer all these to God. He is not a punishing tyrant. Even if you don't love Him, He is ever forgiving and compassionate. He will always be there for you. You will never be alone, ever again," promised Shanti.

Collecting himself and his thoughts, Anveshak asked, "It seems like I might even be able to get God to hear me — but reverence? How do I develop that?"

"Gurudev has said, where there is wonderment, there is a sense of reverence. Before you ask me what that is, let me ask you: Do you

ॐ करूणासागराय नमः Salutations to the ocean of compassion.

He who has realized the Self is friendly toward all living creatures, and he is ever compassionate to all. He offers security of life to all beings. He does not regard anything as his and he is completely free from the notion of egoism.

Discovering one's own Self is the discovery of unconditional compassion. Dive within to embrace all.

see the sun set every day, and does the moon rise every day? Deliberate on those phenomena. How do they happen? You will grow to feel reverence when the answer comes to you. Then there is the air you breathe; without it, you and I are nothing. Whose benevolence is involved in giving us this without pause? Ever wonder about it? Love will seep into you without you even knowing it!"

She made it seem simple and even doable, thought Anveshak. Yet he wanted to know, "You have an ongoing relationship with God. I don't. Are you sure He is going to listen to me?"

Laughing, she quoted Gurudev on his explanation on how God feels about this:

> All those who are with devotion turned toward Me, seeking Me, they get Me. That is all. If they do not seek, I do not go after them. The choice is yours; you are given full freedom.

"God won't come to me without me reaching out...," Anveshak murmured.

ॐ महात्मने नमः **Salutations to the great soul.**

Heat is the nature of fire; therefore, we cannot say that fire creates or generates heat! Similarly, a great soul, wherever he be, whether in a jail among criminals or among devotees in a temple, irresistibly, instinctively, will spread around him an aura of knowledge, light, cheer, joy, and peace. It is his very nature.

Spiritual pursuit is to find the ultimate link that connects all.
Thereafter, no disparity can ever exist.

Reflection: Swami Advayananda

As a young lad of fifteen, I overheard the following conversation between Gurudev and a lady devotee: She blurted out her bottled-up question, a question which I could then not think was possible to ask, and which, as the decades have rolled by, I myself have observed at times raising its vicious hood in my heart, and which I have seen others also grappling with: "Swamiji, what if this whole thing — this Brahman, this Ātman — is a total lie, a lie that has been perpetrated by well-meaning Gurus and their servile śiṣyas. And thus a tradition of falsehood has been perpetuated over the ages?"

The answer that Gurudev gave, and which only Gurudev, a Brahmaniṣṭha, could have given so convincingly, lies firmly imprinted in my heart and has helped me on my dark nights of doubt and confusion: "My dear, do you think I will tell you a lie? Will I ever mislead you? Don't I love you?"

The parents and siblings of Swami Advayananda with Gurudev at Sidhbari. Seated to the left are Swamiji, his sister Brahmacharini Shruti Chaitanya and Roger Warren, also a disciple of Gurudev.

"No Swamiji, it's not that. You love and care for me, I have never doubted that. But this doubt has been torturing me: I am not sure if this whole Vedānta, though so logical, is a big imagination. How do I know that it is really true?"

Gurudev was still for a moment, and then with great compassion flowing from his pellucid eyes, he said, "Look at me. Do you feel, at least sometimes, that there is something remarkable and different about me, something which differentiates me from the rest?"

With no hesitation at all, she replied, "Swamiji, you are very different from all of us. Your love is unconditional, true and universal; you are an embodiment of goodness, so pure and noble, and also absolutely fearless."

Then Gurudev, with great authority, yet with great benevolence, said, "That difference is because of Brahman, which my Guru helped me realize. May you, too, realize this Truth and become free."

This intensely personal approach that Gurudev used to answer her question — unique and yet simple — did not only satisfy her and put her doubt and confusion to naught, but also put back her faith, for immediately a wide smile and joy began to flow from her eyes; she was now the complete antithesis of what she had been a few moments ago.

She had lost the password, but Gurudev had retrieved it for her! Indeed, the super-computer was now back in action.

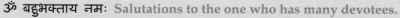

ॐ बहुभक्ताय नमः Salutations to the one who has many devotees.

Gurudev had the ability to connect with each devotee in a unique way, making each one feel important. He addressed each one's need, whether it was about the person's professional, personal, or spiritual challenge.

A mirror has no image of its own, so also a saint who has annihilated the ego!

"Did you get your college degree by doing nothing and staying at home or did you have to work to get it?" Shanti asked rhetorically, sharing how Gurudev had put things in perspective when explaining this to devotees in the U.S.

In this universe, there is this small earth, with a small America in it, with a small California in it. In this small state, there is a Piercy, and in that little Piercy there is Krishnalaya, and in it there is a tent. Inside that little tent, in a corner, you are sitting. That is how insignificant you are compared to this universe. So you cannot expect the Lord of the Universe to turn to you all the time. Instead, you must make an attempt to turn toward Him!

"How do I know if after all this, God will love me?" asked Anveshak. While he understood the rationale offered by Shanti, he was still informed by his experience in the world of binding and bartered love.

"The Lord already loves you just as He loves every creature in this universe. His door is always open. If you open the door of your heart as well, the path will not be narrow. Love Him, that's your choice.

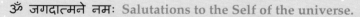

ॐ जगदात्मने नमः **Salutations to the Self of the universe.**

The potmaker makes a pot. But the space in the pot, being itself eternally one with the outer space, is not created or born. Not even the potmaker, after making the pot, pours 'some space' into the pot. He worked in space and, as he molded the pot, he could mold it only with space already inside. Similarly, the body is born in Ātman, the Self — the Soul of the Universe is eternally present in all.

Barring the universal Soul, world is mere matter, a false appearance. For the wise, the world's presence or absence does not matter!

Tracking you down is His responsibility. He did it to me through Gurudev. I learned more about God, through His own manifestation as Gurudev." She continued with tears in her eyes, "Gurudev gave me a glimpse of God's infinite love with His unconditional acceptance. I wonder what I would have been without His grace!?"

As she wiped off the tears that trickled down her cheeks and gazed at the smiling picture of Gurudev on the wall, Anveshak was moved, too, observing her devotion.

Now he wanted to know, "Shantiji, how and when do I begin my dialog with God?"

The gentle lady, the great supplicant of the Lord, said simply, "After work tomorrow, come with me to the temple."

Sādhanā

- Be keenly aware of your place in the world.
- Don't be jaded, observe and enjoy God's creation.
- Strive to be a giver rather than just a receiver of love.

Love is to human hearts what sun is to flowers. Service in this world is the highest prayer. Loving the people around us is the greatest devotion.

X

Learning to Love: Many Modes for the Heart

Anveshak was in a rush to wrap up for the day, Dr. Sevadas noted. Shanti had already called to tell him not to keep Anveshak late at work. Accordingly, he waved the young man off at 5 P.M. and gave him directions to the temple.

Meanwhile, as she waited for Anveshak to come, Shanti bought flowers to offer for the evening pūjā. An enthusiastic Anveshak met her at the temple gate and, after respectfully greeting her, accompanied her to the sanctum to watch the priest conduct the soḍaśa upacāra pūjā. As he viewed the pūjā, his mind was pulled to the time when, as a young boy, his mother would take him to the temple regularly. He had had no idea what the rituals were about and was convinced that they were a sheer waste of time. As he got older, he had resisted the routine and had made sure to have pending assignments to pass off as excuses so that he did not have to accompany his mother. He recalled, with some guilt, how his mother's face would fall whenever he had refused to go. She had never forced him and instead would bring back prasāda from the temple, lovingly uttering God's name while giving it to him. It dawned on him that he had come a long way since then — he was now at the temple voluntarily!

He was jolted from his thoughts with the ringing of the temple bell, and he turned his attention once again to what was transpiring in the sanctum where Lord Kṛṣṇa stood wearing a beatific smile. Anveshak participated in the rituals, standing reverentially during the ārati and accepting the prasāda at its conclusion. But what he was more struck by was the togetherness, the smiles, and the contentment of the devotees around him. Anveshak felt the same sense of quiet that had suffused him at Shantiji's home! With bright eyes, he turned to her as she beckoned him outside to the temple courtyard.

In the setting sunlight, the two seated themselves on a bench and, for a little while, quietly watched devotees go about the temple, chanting, prostrating, ringing bells, and having prasāda. Anveshak was enjoying himself, and if someone had held a mirror in front of his face, he wouldn't have recognized himself — after months, the corners of his mouth were tipped upward in a fleeting smile. He had momentarily forgotten his woes and was, without realizing it, immersed in the magic of the environment.

He decided he would come here often, even every day, if it meant it would bring him this peace. He voiced his resolve to Shanti.

ॐ जीर्णमन्दिरोद्धारकाय नमः **Salutations to the renovator of ancient temples.**
Temples are not portals for the rich to exhibit their money muscles, those who invariably think that they can decide which god to come inside the temple! Temples are to be built on the advice of the saints, and they should decide about the presiding deity and other gods to be installed. With their blessings, temples so built become places to receive blessings from God. Let us first revive the ancient temples before embarking on new ones!

In front of God, all differences with others should be set aside, without which you are not fit to receive even a side glance from Him!

"It's the Lord's presence you feel," she told him ardently, "and also the love that permeates the hearts of the devotees who come here."

After a moment, she asked, "I am so happy that you will be a regular here. But if you are going to come, why don't you do the worship, too?"

Anveshak was taken aback. "I knew it!" he lashed out. "You made it seem simple and now you want me to do the pūjā? I just saw how complicated it was. I don't even know the language." His peace shattered, he stood up, dusting off his pants ready to leave.

Not losing her equipoise, Shanti tugged at his shirt sleeve and forced him to face her. "Love knows no language, Anveshak. Please sit." After meeting her eyes, which were clear in their intent to help, he sat down.

Shanti said, "Love's language is universal. It is the language of the heart. Even animals — and why... even plants and trees — understand this language."

"But still..."

"You may not know Sanskrit, the language you just heard, Anveshak, but really, the All-knowing God can hear and understand anything and everything. You don't have to say the very words that the priest utters. He does it on behalf of all of us. But when you pray, you open your heart for Him to enter into you. Empty yourself of yourself — this is what is known as surrender in prayer."

ॐ उदारहृदयाय नमः **Salutations to the large-hearted one.**

Living as he does in this intimate understanding of Oneness, he cannot but love others as his very own Self. In his case, universal love is not an art to be practiced, not a formality to be followed, nor a goal to be reached; it is his very life breath. Therefore, a saint is a man of true broad-mindedness, which is the natural outcome of kindness, tolerance, and so on. This is the flag of Realization!

The mark of a saint is the universal love that seeks no recognition or reciprocation, and needs no sanction from any religion.

Reflection: Swami Shivatmananda

Pūjya Gurudev Swami Chinmayananda tirelessly preached that each one of us must and should engage in self-study, which leads to immaculate knowledge of the Self. My personal 'sādhanā' consists of daily study of scriptures, a simple pūjā and meditation, and a life of activity dedicated to the feet of Pūjya Gurudev for self-purification.

"Okay," said a slightly sheepish Anveshak and asked, "How do I pray?"

"With devotion," said Shanti. She again quoted Gurudev:

> In the *Bhagavad-gītā*, the Lord confesses: "Those who pray to Me, in them I live and in Me they live." When an individual starts with a spirit of total surrender, praying to his Lord, devotion of its own accord comes to manifest in his heart. When the emotion of devotion increases, the devotee's personality and the infinite nature of the Lord become One. In short, prayer is the spring-field for all devotion.

"What else?"

"That is all that God asks from you."

"Sincere love?"

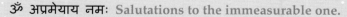

ॐ अप्रमेयाय नमः **Salutations to the immeasurable one.**

However smart we may be in seeing with our eyes, we cannot 'see' our own eyes with our eyes. However tired you may be, you cannot ride even for a yard upon yourself. Similarly, the mind and intellect cannot make the Self an object for their observation and analysis. The moment the Self is detached from the observing mind and the analyzing intellect, they become inert and dead!

Objectifying the Subject (Self) is intellectual suicide. Yet, in that conscious attempt alone, the Self will reveal Its own Nature!

"Yes, with detachment!" She added, "That is all — if you seek only Him and nothing else, not if you ask for your business back or whatever else you may desire. Gurudev calls that 'preying on God.' It would not be praying to God."

"Love for love's sake."

"Yes," affirmed Shanti.

"So, I stand in front of the altar and think only of Him."

"Your practice or sādhanā should not be just at the altar, but at ALL times. In all conditions. And always with love and serenity."

"God demands commitment," Anveshak muttered softly to himself. Coming close to him, Shanti whispered, "Love is commitment."

After this round of rapid-fire questions, Anveshak went silent. Shanti repeated Gurudev's words:

> By rituals, through chanting and singing, through surrender and love, through dedication and prostration, through congregational prayers in especially dedicated and sanctified temples of God, we learn to give up our lesser nature and assert our nobler and diviner possibilities.

In the spirit of nurturing Anveshak, Shanti continued, "The Lord's greatest devotees have told us the many ways, based on our temperament, by which we can cultivate devotion, or bhakti." When Anveshak urged her on, she explained, "By keeping good company

ॐ अनिकेताय नमः: Salutations to the one without an abode.

A devotee has, for himself, a satisfactory shelter only at the seat of the all-pervading Lord, and, therefore, he does not have a sense of possession about his physical abode.

Consciously overcome the sense of possession about all you have in your life.

(satsaṅga) and chanting the Lord's name with them, listening to discourses to hear the glory of the Lord, and remembering, you do it for your benefit, not His."

Anveshak got it. It was similar to what his mother had told him to do through school, so that his academic and personal goals would be bolstered by a like-minded peer group.

"Our love increases when we sing His glory, it is called kīrtanaṁ," continued Shanti.

"Oh. Is that what people are trying to do when they bang on drums and sing as loudly as they can? Developing bhakti? Really?" asked a sarcastic Anveshak, who had not enjoyed the experience as a boy.

"Kīrtanaṁ is sacred, and we sing aloud so anyone can join in and express their devotion to the Lord. You can sing His glory silently at all times in your mind. It is not about going somewhere for an hour to sing and then returning back to a life that is not focused on Him," Shanti clarified.

With the explanation making perfect sense to him, Anveshak thanked Shanti for helping him put aside his disdain for bhajan singers. But he was unclear why one had to go to a temple to develop love for God. Could it not be done at one's own home?

ॐ महर्षये नमः **Salutations to the great seer.**

A sage, experiencing his own Self shining out through every name and form, expressing Its own dynamism through every circumstance, happy or sorrowful, is eternally in unison with harmony and rhythm amidst the discordant noise of life. The greatest potencies, the greatest joys, and the amplest successes in life are his. The heaviest sorrow cannot shake him even a wee-bit.

A sage does not belong to any particular culture, race, religion, or community. He belongs to all. For, all belong to him!

Shanti again used Gurudev's words:

> Companionship of the good (satsaṅga) brings all that is necessary to the seeker. Pursue and try to get these creative contacts which have an infallible influence upon those who are devotees of the Lord.

She added, "How else can you get to know someone better than from their dearest friends? It is the same with God. It is at the temple where you find God's closest friends."

Anveshak recollected how his mother used to come back from the temple with increased love for God. She would have His name on her lips as she cooked dinner and went about her other chores. And when, as a child, he had been afraid of going to bed alone, it was the Lord's name she had whispered into his ears to soothe him.

Shanti said, "When you have Him in your mind, whatever you do in the world is known as pādasevanam. This is also practice of devotion."

"The doctor does sevā," said Anveshak immediately.

Shanti smiled at Anveshak's unflagging support for her husband. "Yes, except here you also combine that kind of service with love for Him and offer whatever you do at His feet."

It was getting quite late and twilight was giving way to nightfall. Ever conscious of her duty as a homemaker and knowing that her husband would be home soon, Shanti rose from the bench. She looked at Anveshak kindly and invited him for dinner again. But he shook his head. He had so much food — for thought!

Sādhanā

- Be steadfast in your goal.
- Surround yourself with people with similar thinking.
- Pray, don't prey.
- Perform every act as an offering to the Lord, remembering Him.

XI

Loving Thyself: God Is in Me

Over the next couple of weeks, Anveshak became increasingly diligent.

He would sit quietly for a few minutes every day in front of the picture of Lord Kṛṣṇa that he now kept at his office desk. He would look at the form and remember and repeat a few of the names of the Lord he had heard the temple priest chant, though he had no idea what they meant. He joined a bhajan group and found himself humming the music even while at work. He went to the temple regularly for the evening pūjā and scoured the web each day to find information on where he could go to attend spiritual lectures.

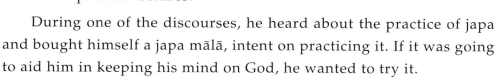

During one of the discourses, he heard about the practice of japa and bought himself a japa mālā, intent on practicing it. If it was going to aid him in keeping his mind on God, he wanted to try it.

He called on Shanti to tell her the new thing he was going to embark on and, once again, they sat in her pūjā room, talking. Encouraging him, she guided him saying, "Make sure when your fingers rotate the mālā, your mind chants steadfastly, and the intellect is aware that it is your offering to Him without expectation of some material benefit."

"I will try to see that my mind doesn't wander off even as I move the beads," he assured her.

"The best way would be to keep your mind on the deity of your heart and chant His name," suggested Shanti.

Though he had already chosen Lord Kṛṣṇa, Anveshak still asked, "Which God should I choose?"

Raising her eyebrows, she reminded him of their earlier conversation, "Whoever you want to become most like. Also, as you continue, consider your relationship with your God," said Shanti.

Knowing Anveshak would not comprehend this, she said, "In life you don't have a choice on the role you will play. The relationships are assigned — daughter, wife, mother, aunt, friend, subordinate, boss, and so on. With Him you get to choose. You can go to God as a friend, lover, parent, or servant."

"Freedom comes with too many choices," grumbled Anveshak.

Shanti laughed, "Time will tell you where your emotions will lead. Don't force it."

Indeed, as the days flew by, Anveshak settled into a routine with his practices. He felt uplifted, experienced joy, but more than anything

---

ॐ आनन्दाय नमः Salutations to the blissful one.

Any attempt of the individual to procure and hold on to sensuous objects is an unconscious act of the individual to bring about the necessary condition in the mind, so that the joyous soul may peep out, beaming its infinite joy. He is nothing but that joyous Self within us!

Attempt to get a glimpse of the infinitely joyful Self by calming the mind and not by fulfilling desires.

else, he felt hopeful. Peace and silence was to be his, too. He knew it!

At work, Sevadas was astounded. Was this the same person who had needed his help not so long ago? Wasn't he the one who had

Rajeshwari, wife of Dr. Pillai, president of CMLA board, offers her devotion to Gurudev.

suggested giving up on rude and not so well-off patients? Now here was Anveshak exhibiting more forbearance and calmness than he himself was capable of.

But unknown to the doctor, the seeker was now experiencing a strange restlessness. His intellect had started questioning his feelings. Was he just bobbing along on a boat of emotions? Shouldn't he be rowing toward a more satisfying destination? Something did not fit. Anveshak's honeymoon with God and the feeling of calm and equipoise was drawing to a close.

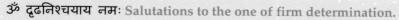

ॐ दृढनिश्चयाय नमः Salutations to the one of firm determination.

To be a seeker only for half an hour in the morning and another half an hour in the evening is not to be a right pursuer of knowledge. Inner revolution cannot be accomplished as a half-hearted hobby, but it can only be the result of a lifelong dedication and a full-time endeavor. He who is ready to live every moment of his life in diligent pursuit of the Real is a true seeker of freedom.

Spirituality is not any special ritual; it is a round-the-clock engagement with the higher Self!

Finally, unable to keep his equanimity, Anveshak burst into Shanti's home one day and with quivering lips cried out, "Why can't I see God?"

Shanti studied the breathless man for a moment. Then she said, "Apart from all the self-effort, we need His Grace."

"Meaning?"

"For an ant that has fallen into a bucket of water, it feels like an ocean. It can't get out without help. Gurudev says that each of us is like that ant. We need His help to rise above our vāsanās and reach Him," said Shanti.

"I thought I was doing that. I have occupied every moment that I have, other than when I am at work, with pūjās, japa, bhajans, and satsaṅgas. He has failed me!" said a desperate Anveshak.

"Has He? Haven't you noticed the changes in you? You have begun to taste the sweetness of divinity and have become greedy for more. You are already enjoying His Grace. Your birth as a human is His Grace, your seeking for Him is His Grace, and, if you receive spiritual guidance, it is also His Grace alone!"

"I do want more."

"Then you need to do more," said Shanti.

As Anveshak looked at her beseechingly, she told him what she remembered from the teachings of Gurudev:

Physically you have evolved as best as possible. Biologically you have reached the highest. Now the next stage of evolution is to readjust the mind. 'Bring your mind to Me, I will adjust and give it back. Surrender the mind, and I will do instant adjustment and give it back to you,' He says. All Gods, in endless number of temples in India, are standing like that, from the day of pratiṣṭhā (installation). Till today they are unemployed and waiting!

"Unless the engine is tuned, my car won't go forward," Anveshak murmured.

"You simply have to surrender your ALL."

"I have surrendered to the idea of surrender," said Anveshak, who had been puzzled for some time now on why anyone would choose to do so. But his recent experiences, having taught him differently, his next question reflected on how he had moved on from the whys and whats. "How do I do that?" he asked.

"By considering Him as the highest goal. All your actions and thoughts should keep sight of this understanding. That's what Gurudev has said."

"Again, how?" demanded an impatient Anveshak, who wanted tangible tools.

How do you reach sleep? Only when you create conditions necessary for it. Your effort is just to create that condition in the mind, and when it is fulfilled, you get sucked into sleep. Similarly, conditions are to be fulfilled in the bosom.

"Gurudev said that?" asked Anveshak when Shanti stopped speaking.

Nodding, she continued in the Master's words:

Whatever you do in this world, offer that to Him. Whatever you eat or consume by any organ, offer those to Him. Whatever responses you give to the outer world, offer those to Him. If you have something in larger amount than you need for survival, share it with Him. Whatever field in which you are consistently putting forth an effort to reach a goal, offer that effort to the Lord. To seek Him, to directly experience His Peace in our bosom, is the peak of devotion.

ॐ अन्तर्यामिने नमः **Salutations to the inner controller.**

Do not remember the Lord merely as personified powers, as Śiva or Viṣṇu, but recognize Him as one who dwells in the heart of every creature. He lends His power for all to act. He energizes everyone. Everything revolves around Him, like the unseen hand that manipulates dolls in the marionette play.

At the place of worship, see His form with your eyes,
see Him Himself with the mind turned within.

"That would be your effort and your devotion. It will earn His Grace, Anveshak."

"But this offering and sharing that I have to do," asked Anveshak, "how do I go about it?"

For once, Shanti was lost with the question, and waited for Anveshak to continue.

"Well, if I want to offer fruits or flowers, I go to the temple. For thoughts, do I have to go somewhere where He is?"

Anveshak's query was so rooted in the physical world, it made Shanti want to laugh. Restraining herself, she said, "Just inward. God is in you."

Sādhanā

- Practice japa to develop bhakti.
- Seek the Lord's Grace.
- Offer everything you do and think at His feet.

ॐ धैर्यप्रदाय नमः Salutations to the giver of fortitude.

A seeker who has turned away from the tragic path of sensuousness and has stepped on to the glorious highway of the Divine, who is prepared to go forward under the guidance of a Guru, with nothing but his independent discriminative reasoning to supply him with mental agility and courage, will surely reach his Goal.

A weakling cannot ever reach spiritual brilliance and total freedom. Courage comes from faith in the Guru and in the path.

XII

Love Is a Many-Splendored Thing

"God is in me?!" Anveshak loudly exclaimed and questioned all at once.

"Undoubtedly," responded Shanti.

"If He is in me, why am I spending my time praying to the idols?"Anveshak demanded to know.

"Gurudev has said, 'Devotion can only be to a *form*. We need something with attributes, properties, and so on, so that we can be devoted to it.'" Shanti continued, "You have been going to the Kṛṣṇa temple. Have you noticed the painting of Anantaśayana — Lord Viṣṇu lying on a multi-headed serpent floating on an ocean?"

"Yes. Lord Viṣṇu is smiling."

"He is content with His great devotee Adi Sesha, the snake. Do you remember what the snake or Ādi Śeṣa looks like?"

Anveshak readily said, "He is coiled to create a bed for Lord Viṣṇu and his hoods hover over the figure of the Lord."

"Now here is what Gurudev said about Ādi Śeṣa and I summarize: The many hoods of the snake represent thoughts. The human mind is capable of thinking in many directions, but Ādi Śeṣa's hoods are always turned inward, toward Viṣṇu. If we turn our mind inward, it will become contemplative. Gurudev also said that the chanting of the thousand names of Lord Viṣṇu through Viṣṇu-sahasranāma-arcanā is like a thousand arrows pointing toward the same target! So the picture of Anantashayana is an instruction to turn all our thoughts to the Lord within. Gurudev said:

> As a sādhanā, we have to go to a spot where for at least ten minutes we can temporarily retreat into the within in ourselves. Throughout the day, we act the part of the mother, the elder, the office, the shopkeeper — but, never are we ever ourselves. To interview oneself by oneself, and to feel our essential oneness with God, is resorting to aloneness (viviktadeśasevanam).

"So, when I worshiped and prostrated to deities, I was invoking this symbolically," Anveshak surmised accurately.

"Yes, in all the rituals that are practiced in a temple this is the underlying message. For example, in a Lord Śiva temple, you will notice a pot of water hung above the Śivaliṅga with a hole pierced at the bottom from which a continuous flow of water gently falls on the Śivaliṅga. This is to indicate that our thoughts should be a steady stream always directed toward Him alone."

ॐ आत्मस्वरूपाय नमः Salutations to the one of the nature of the Self.

You cannot see That which is the witness of vision; you cannot hear That which is the hearer of the hearing; you cannot think That which is the thinker of thought; you cannot know That which is the knower of knowledge. That is your Self which is within all.

The Self is the subject of all experiences. Yet, it is not subject to experience by any other.

Reflection: Mimi Robins

Circumstances and environments are provided by a kindly Lord for our own individual growth. We can reach to them in a joyous mood of humble surrender or revolt against them, in vain, creating despair and sorrow in ourselves.

Be a witness. Smile away. Hold on to faith in yourself and in the final justice and victory of His span of growth.

Gurudev shares a light moment with Mimi Robins in Boston.

ॐ निरञ्जनाय नमः **Salutations to the taintless one.**

In the terminology of philosophy, a mind that is fully agitated is considered as impure. The steady mind, 'agitationless' and alert, is called a pure mind. In order to penetrate into the deeper depths of the spiritual significances in the scriptural texts, it is unavoidable that one should have a certain amount of mental serenity.

Purity of mind is neither mind with good thoughts nor the absence of mind. It is a mind in contemplation, with no experience of distraction.

Anveshak was amazed. So much symbolism lay in all that he had so far dismissed as empty idolatry and rituals!

Shanti continued, "The Mouse in front of Lord Gaṇeśa's idol, Garuda in front of Lord Viṣṇu, Nandi in front of Lord Śiva, the peacock in front of Lord Karthikeya — they represent ultimate devotion. Even animals transformed into devotees because of their unbroken attention on the Lord. They became the vehicles of the Lord. Similarly, your mind can become His vehicle! Understand, Anveshak, that in your quest, wherever He may be, He is your only shelter." Shanti knew that grasping this information was easier than actually practicing it. After all, she herself continued to struggle in her journey to the feet of the Lord.

Satisfied for the moment, Anveshak returned to his apartment. He promised himself that he would strive to practice what Gurudev had said.

ॐ यतात्मने नमः **Salutations to the one of self-control.**

Unless a seeker has come to feel an irresistible urge to know the nature of the Self and to experience as the Self the fullness of life, he will not find in himself the required sense of introvertedness, moral courage, intellectual conviction, mental heroism, psychological guts, and spiritual nerve to dam the outward flow of his senses and thus send the stream of attention in him back again to its very source, the Self. Indeed, such full-blown men are rare in any generation.

In the material world, extroversion is a necessary attribute for knowledge, while for wisdom, introversion is a mandatory prerequisite!

He struggled. He needed to constantly remind himself to stay on the prescribed path so he could feel the presence of God. He had been a businessman, who had lived by rationale and logic, and he had come to deeply admire the flawless reasoning in the teachings and writings of Swami Chinmayananda. Yet, there was a wide gap between his understanding and his everyday experiences.

On some days, he simply quarreled with God, especially when he saw terminally ill patients come to the doctor's office. His heart ached for their well-being. At those moments his doubts resurfaced: Did God even exist?

There were other days when he felt His touch in the silence that he experienced. In those singular moments, his mind had been completely in the present, remembering only the Lord. In those moments of surrender of body and mind, the flashes of joy were unparalleled. His heart was filled with love for the Lord, for everything, and for everyone around him. In those times, he believed God undoubtedly existed!

Anveshak was getting more and more introspective. He realized the quiet mind gave him joy and also allowed him to think. He liked that — the ability to get some answers by himself. The only trouble was he was easily distracted. While during the practice of japa he would feel that he had mastered the mind; at other times, he was unable get a handle on his thoughts — one thought would lead to another, and he

ॐ श्रुति-पारगाय नमः Salutations to the knower of the Śruti.

Teachers of Vedānta accepted the declarations of the Vedas as eternal aspects of the One Truth because of the bona-fide character and temperaments of the Saints who declared them. Later on, for those who wanted more logic and reason, we have a number of verses that support the assertions. The Mastery includes the authentic interpretation of Truth as well as the logic behind It.

Truth is a fact that is seen with the eyes of faith. Let not mere logic blindfold your eyes!

would find himself getting hemmed in by the terrible memories of his 'failed' past.

His mind obviously lacked discipline. DISCIPLINE! How was he to acquire this?

Sādhanā

- ✐ Be strong in your faith in the One.
- ✐ Learn from the form you worship.
- ✐ Trust that you will find your way.

Where individuality is thus merged in His sacred temple of Love, universality starts, the experience of the infinite in us unfolds.

Dhyāna Yoga

Corralling the Mind

XIII

Intertwined: Body and Mind

Anveshak was sitting in the temple hall with his regular bhajan group, showering his love on the Lord, when he was abruptly distracted by some devotees who were loudly talking about the availability of chilled soda on that warm summer evening. His mind picked up on what he had heard and from there it was all downhill.

With his thoughts scattered, he became suddenly and intensely aware of his body and the discomfort from the heat in the temple hall. His thoughts careened even further: annoyance with the temple management for not having the air conditioning on, the volunteers and the devotees' disruptions; none of these thoughts had anything to do with the Lord, whose glory he was singing.

When he recognized how he had mentally vented, he was left thunderstruck by how far his mind had wandered even as he sat in front of the Lord's image. This was so wrong!

As he sat there exasperated, it occurred to him that despite the weeks of japa he had fervently engaged in, his mind had remained distracted: he was usually not completely focused during the length of a pūjā and his attention span while reading about the playfulness of Lord Kṛṣṇa or the magnificence of Lord Rāma often fell short of what it should have been. Sometimes, his mind would even wander off toward the time when he had despaired of living.

He asked himself if he was trying to escape from the direst memories rather than confronting them. Was he trying to feel secure by not thinking about the world?

As he frequently did during such times of introspection, he recalled the picture of Gurudev, which hung on Dr. Sevadas's office wall. And as he had often experienced, he strangely found his restlessness decreasing. He just did not understand it.

What he did not realize was that with all his new activities and understanding, he had grown to be more sensitive than he had ever been before. Even trivial matters triggered anxious feelings in him. Perhaps, he was expecting the transformation to happen too quickly?

What he did get was that he yearned for the silence which he experienced when he felt connected with God. It was the only time he was truly, truly, happy.

But right now, he was frustrated.

He got up and midway through the hour-long bhajan session slipped out of the hall. He made his way to the sanctum and prostrated to Lord Kṛṣṇa, silently remonstrating with him. He got no great flash of insight and yet was able to temporarily soothe his troubled heart.

Anveshak slowly walked out to the temple courtyard and sat under the jacaranda tree in the cool evening air. His attention was captured by a lone figure in the far left of the vast courtyard. From the

ॐ एकस्मै नमः Salutations to the one alone.

The goal is in realizing that the Self in us is the same Self in everything and every being. This realization of the divine nature of man, individually experienced, each for himself, is the only method by which we can be liberated from the bondages of intellectual restlessness, mental agitations, and physical cravings.

The Ultimate or the Absolute has to be One; it is the same that is within each of us, trying to rediscover Itself!

distance, he wasn't sure if the lady even breathed. He stared transfixed, waiting for movement. As the minutes ticked by, Anveshak unable to resist, slowly approached her. In the midst of the cacophony of bells ringing and children running, she simply sat cross-legged with her eyes closed — motionless. He had to get to almost touching distance to see the rise and fall of her breath. On noting this, he exhaled loudly, only then realizing he had been holding his breath, partly in amazement and partly out of worry, but he knew not for what.

Stepping back, he decided to see how long the lady would be able to sit undisturbed. The crowds in the temple were thinning out, and the lady showed no inclination to open her eyes. Was there a problem? Should he be worried and call for help? As he debated with himself, she brought her palms together in prostration (namaskāra).

Anveshak was caught off guard when she opened her eyes and looked straight at him. Like the proverbial kid caught with his hand in the cookie jar, he shifted from one leg to another — was she going to think the worse of him for staring? But she just looked at him steadily and when he didn't seem inclined to talk, quirked an eyebrow at him.

ॐ देहातीताय नमः **Salutations to the one who is beyond body consciousness.**

One who is striving to learn the art of meditation must slowly and carefully develop in himself an attitude of holding himself neutral in all receptions of stimuli and in his responses to them. A man of reflection does not identify with these. They may go on at the physical level because of the prārabdha of the body.

Going beyond the body does not mean one should ignore it; take care of the body, but do not get carried away by it!

"Huuhhhh…," was his inarticulate response.

Chuckling, the lady asked, "Can I help you?"

"How can you sit still for this long?" The question popped out of Anveshak before he could formulate it properly.

"Why? Is that a problem?"

Anveshak shook his head vigorously."How is it even possible?"

"By controlling the body," she said.

"How do you do that?"

"By controlling the mind," was her reply.

"How do you control the mind?"

"By overcoming thoughts about the body," she said.

"How do you overcome those thoughts?"

"By disciplining the mind," she said.

Anveshak looked at her dubiously. This lady spoke in circles. Just as he was about to tell her that, she said, "By the way, I am Damayanti, a yoga instructor. I was meditating."

Raising his hands in a namaskāra, Anveshak introduced himself and asked, "Is it something that I can learn to do?"

She looked at him with curiosity. "You have to practice it. You are welcome to come to my studio where I teach yoga," she said.

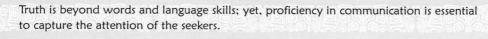

ॐ आङ्ग्ल-भाषा-विदुत्तमाय नमः Salutations to the best among the knowers of the English language.

Gurudev was asked why he was successful. His answer was: "There are hundreds of saints who are successful in their teaching work. They are working in villages and in various monasteries at remote places. Because I come to cities, and talk in English, it looks as though I am more successful than others!"

Truth is beyond words and language skills; yet, proficiency in communication is essential to capture the attention of the seekers.

After settling on the time and day on when he would meet her, Anveshak left for home. He called Shanti to tell her that the next evening he would not be going to the temple but would head instead to meet yoginī Damayanti.

Gently encouraging him, she advised, "Find your way, Anveshak. But don't forget what you have learned so far. Practice all you know as building blocks for your path toward the Lord."

Touched, Anveshak thanked her. Early the next morning, he received a call back from Shanti. "Anveshak, before you go to the yoga studio, will you please read what Gurudev has said about preparations for meditation?" she asked. On his ready assent, she said, "I will send some books through my husband to work. Please take them from him."

During the lunch break, Anveshak sat down to eagerly read the book Sevadas had brought from home. He read what Gurudev said on how one should sit for meditation:

The posture recommended for meditation is that you sit on a flat cushion or folded blanket with your maximum base firmly on the seat, the vertebral column erect and perpendicular to the ground. There is no regulation as to how the legs should rest. Most important is that you keep the legs in a position that offers minimum strain. Folding the legs has a physiological effect, for in that position the least amount of blood will flow to the lower half of the body, thus making a larger amount of blood available for the capillaries of the brain. During meditation the intellect has to function intensely, and this intense functioning is probably facilitated when a larger amount of blood is made available for the brain.

Reflection: Swamini Gurupriyananda

Gurudev wrote in 1990, on the day of Holi: "I want you to be the colorless upon which we see all colors superimposed." Later, the same year he wrote again,"In Gujarat they dance around a mud pot which has holes all around and a lighted lamp inside. It represents prāṇa expressing through music. This light sport is Īśvara, whose light beams out through all sense organs, mind, intellect equipment to illumine the (Objects, Emotions, Thoughts) world of time and space."

Anveshak was impressed with the scientific reasoning but, really, to just sit down, was so much instruction necessary? It was as though Gurudev was listening to him, for he found his answer soon enough:

> You can never express love or devotion with your sleeves rolled up and your fists clenched tight. ...Not only does your mental condition advertise its nature upon the physical body, but the position and condition of the physical body, to a large extent, determine and control your mental attitude. There is a close relationship between physical posture and mental condition.

Anveshak read on, about what should be done once seated:

> Keep the back, neck, and head in one straight line. Do not lean. Chest forward! Vertebral column erect. Trunk, neck, head in one line. With bottom firm and trunk not even moving a millimeter forward or backward, sit! The only movement of the body is due to your breathing. But the margins of the body should be kept like the trunk of a dead tree.

 ॐ धीमते नमः **Salutations to the intelligent one.**
No Guru worth the name will allow their disciples to choke their independent reasoning faculty. The best of Gurus have always endeavored to cultivate a better crop of reasoning in the intellect of their disciples.

God-realization in Vedānta is with the Intellect as the doorway. It is usually locked from inside!

Anveshak delighted in the explanation and the clear guidance of Gurudev. He wasn't sure if he could meditate, but he was definitely going to give it a try. So after another busy day at work with Sevadas, keeping Shanti's words in mind and Gurudev's words in his heart, he reached yoginī Damayanti's studio. It was a large facility, and if the parking lot was any indication, a popular one. After waiting for a few minutes, he was ushered into the presence of the yoginī. After the initial pleasantries she asked:

"Why do you want to meditate?"

"I want to be able to sit still like you and be unbothered by things around me," Anveshak said. He then shared with her Gurudev's instructions on how to be seated.

"Okay, I see it is going to be one step at a time with you," Damayanti smiled. She liked the openness of this young man and his non-pretentiousness. "Why don't you begin with the correct posture as suggested by Swami Chinmayananda?"

Pulling a light cushion toward him on the clean wood floor, Anveshak prepared to sit. Barely five minutes into closing his eyes at the urging of the yoginī, he felt the need to adjust his posture. He scratched an itch on his arm and closed his eyes once more. Now his foot hurt. He shifted. The cushion did not feel soft enough; his bottom needed support. He opened his eyes again. The yoginī was staring at him.

"It is more than just the cushion and your bottom," she told him solemnly.

Sādhanā

🖉 Understand the connection between body and mind.

🖉 At all times, seek!

XIV

Taming the Body: Self-Control

Anveshak sighed. He knew he was in for the long haul if stillness was to be his.

"Where do I begin?" he asked.

"First, there has to be physical discipline," Damayanti explained. "Prepare your body for the meditation seat. It's not like sitting on a couch to daydream."

"You want me to go to the gym first?' asked a clueless Anveshak.

"It is not about flexing muscles or counting your abs. It is about adopting a state of brahmacharya."

He had heard that word before. Wasn't it celibacy?

"I am not married. I am okay," replied Anveshak promptly.

The yoginī almost rolled her eyes in delight. This fellow was going to be fun. "You mentioned Swami Chinmayananda to me earlier. Since that Master's words seem to touch you, why don't you go home and read what he has to say on brahmacharya? We can talk more afterward."

Late that night, while thumbing through the material sent to him by Shanti, Anveshak stumbled on what Gurudev had said:

The physical body longs for contact with the world of objects in order to gain sense gratification. The eyes wish to see beautiful forms and colors, the tongue craves good food, the nose likes to smell pleasant fragrances, and so on. But when we continue to live only for the gratification of our sensual demands, passions multiply and ultimately consume us. To avoid such a condition, discipline, or brahmacharya at the physical level is prescribed.

Pondering on it, and full of questions, Anveshak slept.

The next evening, he was back at the studio.

"So I'm not supposed to relish good food and enjoy the smell of plumerias?" he demanded.

"Nobody said never," rejoined the yoginī, "just do everything in moderation. I believe that Swami Chinmayananda said the same thing in the book you were reading about how to be seated for meditation. Why don't you read that a bit further?"

Anveshak had brought the book along and while browsing further, he found Gurudev's advice:

> Eat whatever comes handy, without creating unnecessary destruction to the living kingdom just for your personal existence, and consume an intelligent quantity which does not load your stomach. This is the golden rule of dieting for a successful meditator.

"Let me understand. If I eat five slices of pizza to fill myself at lunch, now I have to moderate myself and be happy with three pieces?" he asked Damayanti.

"What it means is if you have even a single bite more than the five slices that are required to fill you, you are showing lack of discipline.

ॐ जितेन्द्रियाय नमः Salutations to the master of the sense organs.

All obstacles in meditation are nothing other than the millstones of sensuous appetites, emotional agitations, and desire problems. Once these chains are snapped, a seeker comes to the natural condition of deep meditation, wherein the rediscovery of the Self must be instantaneous and complete.

Mastering the senses is to treat them as servants and never as friends or associates!

It's succumbing to the senses. You don't need it, yet you take it," said the yoginī. "Try to see the difference between need and want."

"I have often overeaten," admitted Anveshak.

"How did you feel after?" asked Damayanti.

"Heavy, overfed and fat," replied Anveshak.

"Sleepy, indolent," added Damayanti. He nodded in agreement.

"How do you feel when you spend eight hours watching TV?"

"Lazy, useless. I get it. Moderation," said Anveshak in response.

"When you don't overdo things, you are disciplined. Brahmacharya is discipline, discipline of the senses," explained the yoginī.

"So I don't need to stop enjoying pizza completely?" Anveshak wanted to be clear.

"Discipline is needed, not denial of the senses," the yoginī said.

"Wouldn't that be quicker?" asked Anveshak.

"In the short run you will feel like total denial works well. But have you noticed what happens to people who go on diets?"

"They usually return to their old habits," agreed Anveshak, but asked, "And if I eat only two slices and stop?"

"You will feel weak, tired, hungry, irritable, and completely unsuitable for the seat of meditation," she continued, "It is not only about food and eating. It is about all sensory indulgences. Listening to music all the time, or even working too much."

ॐ कालातीताय नमः **Salutations to the one beyond time.**

Time itself is a concept of the intellect. When the 'first thought' arose in the Infinite, there was no concept of 'time.' Time is the interval between two thoughts. Identifying with the first thought, the Cosmic Mind allowed the second, third, and fourth thoughts in a continuous procession. Therefore, when the first thought arose, time was not yet born.

In meditation, minimize thoughts and reach to one; stay there until it disappears in No Time!

Anveshak's thoughts veered toward Dr. Sevadas. Wasn't he breaking the rules of brahmacarya? He had never noticed the doctor even sitting in his room quietly. He was always working. The doctor had never mentioned meditation to him. Perhaps because he had never done it!

The yoginī continued to illustrate the point. "The same with television. If you keep thinking you shouldn't watch TV because you are about to become a meditator, the first thought that will come to your head when you sit down to meditate will be: "I've missed seeing my favorite TV show!" When you watch too much, not only is your body in a state of lethargy, but your mind too has taken in so many sights, sounds, and emotions that it can't be alert for meditation."

What he heard made sense to Anveshak. "Do you have any advice on how I can practice this moderation?" he asked.

"Observe yourself at every moment," came the reply that sounded simple but was to pose several practical challenges for Anveshak over the coming days.

He walked the tightrope between disciplined need and suppression. He tilted one way one moment and the opposite in the next. Was he really so out of control, he wondered. Yet, throughout this phase, he did two things: The first was to copiously read Gurudev's writings on

---

Reflection: Acharya Gaurang Nanavaty

Gurudev's tireless repetition of the watchwords "Quiet–Alert–Vigilant" is the key to a successful sādhanā. One must first keep the mind quiet – a quiet mind is capable of quick and clear focus. Then, the minute a seeker feels like compromising in his sādhanā, his quiet and now alert mind will notice. Thereon, the seeker will refocus his efforts and become vigilant, not allowing the mind to derail from the chosen path.

the subject. In the process, he found yet another gem that added more clarity to his perspective:

> Brahmacharya, or abstinence from any sense indulgence in thought, word, or deed, is a necessary practice. …Any excessive indulgence through any of the sense organs — be it excessive eating, loose talking, or listening to scandal — would mean breaking the rules of brahmacharya.

And, second, no matter what, Anveshak would sit in a corner of his balcony with closed eyes observing his body just as Gurudev had suggested:

> Relaxation before meditation is effected through a process called thought-massage, by which the meditator, with closed eyes, sends his thoughts consciously down his body, mentally massaging and relaxing every muscle.…When the body is relaxed, you will find that you feel heavier against the seat, or that the seat presses upward with increased insistence. …The gross weight and tensions of the body no longer pull your attention to the physical plane. You have entered the meditation seat, with all the preliminaries of body adjustment completed.

Anveshak found himself enjoying all this reading, and then practicing what he had read. He felt each suggestion that Gurudev had imparted — that in a state of relaxation the body would feel like it's been suspended from the shoulders just as a coat hangs from a hanger. Gurudev had promised, and he experienced it: The gross weight and tensions of the body no longer pulled attention to the physical plane.

He happily shared his feelings with the yoginī.

"You are able to sit without moving?" she asked.

Grinning, Anveshak answered, "Yes!"

"How do you feel, when you are in the meditation seat?"

"Calm," said Anveshak.

"And when you open your eyes and get up?"

"I wish I could stay that way forever," Anveshak murmured.

"Has the world around you changed when you get up after a good night's sleep?" the yoginī asked. Anveshak had by now understood that even though her questions at first sounded like they were off target, they circled their way back to their original point of discussion. "It hasn't," he replied.

"When you wake up, do the same problems remain?" asked the yoginī. "It is the same with your state of meditation. When you sit still, you feel a relative quiet, but when you open your eyes, you face the same issues as before and the calmness vanishes," she explained.

"Now what?" Anveshak asked.

"You have learned to control the body, but now shift your attention more firmly to your mind," advised Yoginī Damayanti.

"Self-control of the mind?" he asked to be sure he understood.

"What has stopped you from overeating?" she asked, and without waiting for his reply went on, "It is your mind that told your body that it did not desire excess food. The mind controlled the body's desire and the body was controlled. Now imagine if the control center, your mind, can be told to be calm and happy at all times."

ॐ तपस्विने नमः: Salutations to the ascetic.

When an individual reduces his indulgences in the world outside through conscious self-denials at the body level, he gains more energy within himself and applies the newfound energy for the purpose of self-development — this process is called tapas.

When practiced unwillingly, self-denial is self-torture, leading to anger and frustration; it cultivates patience and strength when practiced intelligently.

He was supposed to talk his mind into being happy? Really? "And I am sure you know and will tell me how I can tell my mind to do this," smirked Anveshak.

"Sarcasm doesn't become you, Anveshak," said the yoginī tartly.

"So my mind has to tell itself to be happy?" he asked, a bit chastened, but disbelief raised its head again, "Just keep repeating 'I am happy' and it will happen?"

Yoginī Damayanti said, "Don't underestimate the power of repetition. Have you seen what Swami Chinmayananda has to say about it?"

"About repetition?"

"Try the word japa," she said.

His discovery of self-control, which the yoginī had enjoined upon him to understand, turned him more and more toward Gurudev's words. He soon came upon these words:

> Every attempt at living in self-control — in all our contacts with the outer world, wherein all the efforts are dedicated for the high purpose of evolving ourselves into a diviner being — is called tapas. From pilgrimage and fasting to japa and dhyāna — all spiritual endeavors at self-control are different types of tapas.

ॐ स्थित-प्रज्ञाय नमः: Salutations to the one of steady wisdom.

Equanimity is the essence of perfection, and a Man of Wisdom is in perfect steadiness and balance. He craves nothing, nor does he strive to acquire anything new. To have or not have, both are equal to him, because he is beyond both, living a life of inward peace, which is totally independent of all environments.

Wisdom is not about how much you know, but how deeply you know yourself. Wisdom is not taught, it is caught!

Japa was self-control? He had been rotating the japa-mālā since Shanti had introduced it to him. He thought it was a way of showing love for the Lord. How was this discipline? One of Gurudev's books that Shanti had provided gave him the answer:

> Japa generally enchants the unwary practitioner into unproductive thought-wanderings. If the student is not diligent and does not arrest his thoughts, it is possible that his japa will cause frustration and stupor. The need to sleep is strong because a mind in japa is a mind at rest. Bad temper happens because of two reasons — suppression of tendencies and fatigue.

Anveshak was stunned. That was exactly his problem. He had been suppressing his thoughts! Japa should not be an escape from problems. It should be an intelligent substitution and focus, he realized.

He read further:

> Regularity and sincerity are the secrets of success in any spiritual endeavor, including Japa Yoga. Guard the mind against all excesses and make it immune to selfishness and passion. Watch how imperceptibly the mind ties itself down to things, beings, happenings, and circumstances by its own unintelligent attachments. Approach your japa in surrender. The potential strength of blessing that lies dormant in japa will then be invoked.

Japa is the surrender of the mind? SURRENDER, once again!

Sādhanā

- Practice moderation in thought and action.
- Don't suppress, sublimate.

XV

Cultivating the Mind: Pure Thoughts

The following evening, Anveshak spoke again with the yoginī, "How long have you been doing meditation?" he asked her.

"You don't 'do' meditation, you can only practice to reach the State of Meditation," she said.

"Okay then, for how long have you been in this 'state'?" asked Anveshak, drawing quotation marks in the air with his fingers.

"I think the relevant question would be: How long did it take for me to get here?" the yoginī replied and paused. "A very long time and a very short time," she continued.

Anveshak and the yoginī by now had an established pattern in their communication — he would ask, and she would give answers that spun his head with their circuitousness. He would then get acerbic, and she would bait him with a response that got him thinking.

So, true to form, with a touch of sarcasm, he said, "I am sure the long and short mean the same thing." The yoginī was unfazed.

"When I sat and shifted and moved restlessly like you, it felt like forever to get to a better state," she explained.

"So when did it feel like it was quick?" he asked.

"When I first felt the flash of inner silence," she said.

"And you felt it after two years, three?" Anveshak wanted a timeline.

"Three years ago I went on a pilgrimage with a Swamiji from Chinmaya Mission to Mt. Kailash. It had to be the most difficult journey I have ever under taken. I was breathless; the altitude gave me headaches, and I was always cold. Putting one foot in front of the other and pulling myself forward to be as physically close to the Lord as possible was painful and demanding," she said with her eyes closed.

Anveshak waited silently for her to continue."And yet, I knew I could not and would not give up. I kept telling myself that the journey was worth it."

"And was it…for you, I mean?"Anveshak asked softly.

The yoginī opened her eyes. "It was searing," she said simply.

"So you are telling me the journey was worth the goal," Anveshak surmised.

The yoginī nodded her head."Despite the major difficulties that the body faced, it listened to the mind that repeatedly told it to go forward. I was singularly focused on doing the circumambulation (parikramā) of the holy Kailash mountain."

"So repetition brought focus to the mind, and you were able to get to where you wanted to be," Anveshak said.

"I was guided by Swamiji, who has been my inspiration in understanding the mind," the yoginī said.

Anveshak thought for a moment. Yoginī Damayanti was obviously not going to divulge the length of time it was going to take for him to

ॐ छिन्नसंशयाय नमः Salutations to the one free from doubts.

To have a doubt and to come to a decision about it are the two equal yokefellows in the process of intelligent living. That is, the doubt must be mine, and the ultimate understanding must also be mine, so that I may experience the disappearance of my doubt. He who helps a seeker in this process is the Guru.

Unconfirmed information is doubt. Confirm it with the one who is firm about the provided information!

get to the State of Meditation. A state she seemed to be so easily able to slip into. He moved on, "Will your Swami be able to tell me how long it will take for me to perfect meditation?"

The yoginī thought about it for a moment. While Anveshak's questions seemed very pedantic and uninformed, the reality was that he was ready and deserved deeper answers which she herself was not likely to have. She also remembered what Swamiji had once told her about meditation, "Most people are interested either to practice without knowing the true purpose, or to listen to theory and never practice. A true seeker is not just curious. He wants to know so that he does not doubt himself, halfway."

If the nature of the mind and how to tame it had to be explained, there could be no one better to do it than Swamiji. Unfortunately, he was out of town that week, so she called Professor Vidyadhar, a fellow Kailash yātri with whom she had struck up a friendship, impressed by his insight and knowledge.

Vidyadhar had taught philosophy for several years, but a special interest in Vedānta was sparked in him only after he had heard Swami Chinmayananda speak at the university. Gurudev's stirring discourse on the *Bhagavad-gītā* had clearly shown the professor, the relevance of the ancient scripture to modern challenges. Vidyadhar had been hooked. From then on, he considered Swami Chinmayananda his Guru and like the scholar he was, read voraciously the master's work.

Now, after hearing Damayanti, he set aside his misgivings about the dedication and capability of some young man wanting to meditate and agreed to meet with Anveshak.

"Meditation is not for beginners," he said brusquely and without any preamble when he arrived a short while later at the studio. "Gurudev has said there are pre-conditions."

Anveshak went through a multitude of emotions. One was of amazement that here was yet another person talking about Swami Chinmayananda — it was getting to be more than a coincidence. He tucked the thought away for now, struggling with the more predominant feeling of dejection knowing that he was a beginner. Meditation might not be for him; however, he was eager to hear what the preconditions might be.

The professor had dealt with students all his life. He correctly read Anveshak and rephrased encouragingly, "Yoginī Damayanti tells me you have cultivated love for the Lord and you also serve at a doctor's office."

ॐ गीता-ज्ञान-यज्ञ-प्रचारकाय नमः Salutations to the propagator of the *Gītā*.

The ideal nature of all true students of the *Bhagavad-gītā* should be a glorious synthesis of both the Spiritual Knowledge expressed in their equipoise and character, and the dynamic Love expressed through their service to mankind and their readiness to sacrifice.

Knowledge is sustained by Love, and in turn, Love enhances the Knowledge. Spirituality is complete only when both head and heart unite in service.

When Anveshak nodded his head in acknowledgement, Professor Vidyadhar pushed his glasses up his nose and with concentration quoted Gurudev:

> Beginners must strive to make their mind and intellect quiet, calm, serene, single-pointed, and sincere. This is achieved through devotion and consequent surrender of one's actions at the altar of reverence. At this stage, the mind of the individual is ready for meditation.

Anveshak brightened.

"Damayanti also tells me, you have learned to control your body. You are on your way, young man!" said the professor, "Work on your mind and don't worry about the time taken. It is not the same for all."

"How come?"

"Because what you are trying to understand is different from the study of a bachelor's degree, which my students complete in four years. Even there, the learning and understanding students leave college with is uniquely their own. It is shaped by their unalloyed and distinctive experiences. The path of your inquiry is shaped not only by your present experiences or just your immediate past, but all your previous births too!" said Vidyadhar.

ॐ साधवे नमः **Salutations to the Saint.**

A Self-realized Saint's activities do not touch him at all since he is not the actor; the actions only flow through him. Such a truly great one becomes not a doer of actions, but serves as a glorious instrument for the Lord's will to express Itself.

Everyone wants to become somebody in life, but a true seeker seeks to become nobody. As he advances toward his goal, the Lord takes over.

"I am a collection of all that?" asked Anveshak.

The professor was pleasantly surprised with Anveshak's thinking ability. "Yes! Do you know how that manifests itself?"

"The way my mind thinks," answered Anveshak tentatively. He was used to asking the questions, not providing answers.

"And what is this thing that you call mind?" asked the professor.

"Where my thoughts are," said Anveshak after ruminating on the question briefly.

Reflection: Rose Ann Blau

Over the years, Rose Ann Blau had the good fortune of receiving letters of advice from Pūjya Gurudev: Don't expect progress in meditation overnight. It will come to us in its own time. Honestly try to be as quiet as possible in meditation. Don't take disturbances seriously. Ignore them. Never protest against their arrival but see that your attention doesn't float away with the thought currents. Stay in His thoughts and allow dissimilar thought currents to dance around you. Be regular in daily study and meditation. Whenever free, learn to contemplate upon those beautiful verses explaining 'the things to be known.'

Gurudev with devotee Rose Ann Blau in the U.S.

So long as we expect the Experience, it will escape us. Just BE in meditation.

In response, the professor quoted Gurudev again:

> When we think about what the mind is, we always associate it with thoughts. However, we cannot say that the mind is thought. If that were true, we would have to say that we have many different minds, since few thoughts remain for more than a flashing moment.

Anveshak asked, "If the mind is not thoughts, then what is it?"

"Gurudev calls it a phantom power."

"It doesn't exist!" Anveshak felt he was reeling.

"When a river dries up and leaves in its wake small bodies of water, does the river exist?" asked the professor.

"No."

"Gurudev gave us the river analogy for our thoughts. When the thought-river continues to flow without interruption, it creates the idea that there is a powerful mind. Uncontrolled, our thoughts create a disastrous flood."

That's what had happened to him at the Golden Gate Bridge, when he had rushed, unheeding and blind to everything, toward the ledge, Anveshak figured.

"And when controlled, our thoughts reveal the inherent calmness," the professor said.

"Where do thoughts come from?" asked Anveshak.

"From your response to objects," said Vidyadhar.

"Ah, that's why Damayantiji kept telling me to control my senses," Anveshak concluded.

"If the water is dirty, the river is dirty. If our thoughts are agitated, what we know as the mind is stressed. If our thoughts are impure, our mind enshrines those base values. So Gurudev has said that we should reduce our quantity of thoughts with selfless service, improve their quality with love, and change the direction of our thoughts by aiming them toward higher realms," the professor explained.

This was all very illuminating for Anveshak but he wanted clarity on something else. "You said I am made up of all my past births and experiences. If I sit down for meditation, will my thoughts be influenced by that too?"

Even yoginī Damayanti was keen to hear the answer.

Professor Vidyadhar provided Gurudev's explanation:

> Humans function on three levels — the conscious, subconscious, and the unconscious. The conscious level is where all the thoughts have been fully realized. The subconscious level is where all the dashed hopes and crumpled emotions are held and the unconscious level is what we don't even know about but act out as impulses; it is driven by the vāsanās accumulated over all past births.

"So much baggage," mumbled Anveshak. Yoginī Damayanti nodded in agreement.

"What do you do at the airline counter when they tell you that you have excess baggage?" Professor Vidyadhar asked.

"I try to reduce what I have in the bag."

ॐ सुमनसे नमः **Salutations to the one of good mind.**

Once, someone asked Gurudev if he was ever tired of having people around him all the time. He answered, "Only if there is hate in the heart does one get tired of people. Do you ever get tired of your arms and legs? Do you ever want them to go away?"

Seeing oneself in all is the culmination of Self-realization. The world is a mirror, and everyone who comes in front of you is only yourself!

"How?" asked the professor.

"By throwing unwanted stuff out."

"Nature does that for you. Haven't you been the most powerful? Told off your worst enemy? Married the most beautiful woman? Been the envy of everyone?"

"In my dreams!" laughed Anveshak.

"Precisely. When you sleep, the conscious which deals with outside objects in wakeful moments is at rest, and the subconscious creates these beautiful dreams for you. In your dreams, many thoughts play out and get tossed out."

"So I need to sleep more to ready myself for control of the mind?" Anveshak wondered.

That didn't go down well with the professor. Seeing the beginning of a scowl, the yoginī jumped in, "I know you do pūjā and bhajans, you could consider how you feel when you are doing that," she interjected quickly.

"Lighter and happier," Anveshak said.

"That's because the conscious mind has been reined in and the subconscious thoughts have been shown the exit door as they are irrelevant for your spiritual growth," said the Professor.

"So, I have to work on quieting the conscious mind," said Anveshak.

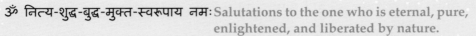

ॐ नित्य-शुद्ध-बुद्ध-मुक्त-स्वरूपाय नमः Salutations to the one who is eternal, pure, enlightened, and liberated by nature.

When we pass from one plane of consciousness into another, we cannot ever smuggle anything into the new from the earlier. Thus, when the ego ends in spiritual awakening, when the experience of the pure Brahman is opened up, there is total merger of the entire world earlier experienced by the ego. Through meditation, when one transcends and merges in the Absolute, the 'roar of realization' is the experience of the eternal, pure, blissful Freedom!

Ego alone is the experiencer of the states of waking, dream, and deep sleep. With the end of ego, there is only a continuous, endless, pure bliss of the Self!

The yoginī and the professor exchanged knowing smiles, looking pleased.

"Without all that excess baggage you can begin to check into the flight," said the professor.

"Taking only the essentials," chimed in the yoginī.

"The essentials....?" repeated Anveshak.

"A positive mind," said the yoginī. "Our behavior is not only about what we should not do for self-control but also what we should do."

Professor Vidyadhar quoted Gurudev:

> A positive mind does, rather than just refrain from doing. Suppression of desires is replaced by positive desireless-ness. A positive mind does not merely eschew jealousy, but rejoices in the prosperity of others; it does not merely refrain from hating, but it loves; it does not just tolerate, but it forgives; it does not merely desist from telling lies, but it always speaks the truth; it is not only free of greed, but it is generous. A positive mind is poised in peace, free from delusions, seeking the good of all and flows with unbroken love for everyone.

"Goodness! If I were to practice all these noble qualities I would be Lord Rāma!" exclaimed Anveshak.

"Not all, but begin with one at least" said the Professor.

"If I was to begin with one value and live it to its fullest potential, which one should I practice?"

Professor Vidyadhar said, "Gurudev said if we practice one value fully, the others will follow. He considered ahiṁsā, or non-injury, as a cornerstone for development of the mind, like a moral code. Let me share what he said:

> Ahiṁsā does not simply mean non-killing or non-injury, at the
> physical level. It is to be understood as a mental attitude regarding
> our relationship with others. Non-injury is the spirit that should
> dominate the realm of our motives.

Anveshak remembered a statement from one of the discourses he had heard on the *Bhagavad-gītā* where Kṛṣṇa declared: He is my devotee who hates none! He saw the connection now. Love was non-injury not only on the physical plane but the mental one too.

"Now you are ready to take off!" exclaimed the yoginī.

Back home, Anveshak was concerned about the practice of ahiṁsā. He had not forgiven his fiancée. But now, he no longer wanted to wallow in the feelings of hate or even dislike. He wanted to forgive, but how?

He thought deeply and hours later the solution came to him: "I am not able to forgive because I have been thinking that my failures and disappointments were caused by people around me. In my subconscious mind, the emotional pain I experienced has left an unhealed wound. I should overcome this by surrendering to His will. If I have been chanting His name while doing japa, why do I not believe that He can heal my wounds?"

Surrender is true ahiṁsā. He had found a new dimension to the word SURRENDER.

Sādhanā

> Observe the quality of your thoughts.
> Reduce mental agitations caused by contact with external objects.
> Practice surrender to a Higher Power.

XVI

Meditation: Sensing the Void

With so much to think about, Anveshak sat down on the floor, with his back resting against the wall by the small altar in his home that Shanti had helped him build. This place had become a haven for him. He had skipped going to the yoga studio or temple and instead just sat pondering on all he had heard from Professor Vidyadhar and yoginī Damayanti.

He had been a businessman and did not like gray areas. He took stock of his current status. What he wanted: peace and happiness. Solutions that his new friends had offered: serve the community, love the Lord, gain self-control over mind and body and get ready to meditate. His experience: the first made him feel good, the second soothed his heart, the third he had not yet tried fully.

It was time to get the tools for meditation. He had to agree that the whole process was really very scientific, and that appealed to him greatly.

He remembered the words of Gurudev from one of the books he had read:

Just as science has sought to discover the nature and behavior of things of the world, philosophy has been struggling, from the beginning of time, to discover the contents of the world within man. In contrast to the Western philosophy, which is essentially a 'view of life,' the philosophy of the Hindus, besides being a 'view of life,' is also a 'way of life.' The six main schools of philosophy — every one of them — has a complete and clear prescription of a technique, following which the practitioner can be assured of achieving his or her spiritual goal.

Anveshak now realized that what he was seeking was spiritual fulfillment, and not just a temporary solution for his immediate problem.

The following weekend, Anveshak found himself at the small park adjoining the yoga studio, observing with some fascination, the yoginī seated on the green grass in a meditative posture. Professor Vidyadhar, a regular early morning jogger, seeing Anveshak from a distance, joined him.

"How do you come out of meditation?" Anveshak launched the question at the professor before he had even seated himself.

The professor laughed and without missing a beat asked, "Do you come and go from your dreams and sleep?"

When Anveshak shook his head, Professor Vidyadhar said, "Gurudev has said it is a movement of consciousness from one state into another. It is not a movement in space or time. For example, you can get into a plane in Los Angeles, fly for eighteen hours, and finally reach Delhi. You may also travel in your dreams. But do you see the difference between the two types of travel?"

"In the first example, I have taken off in one place and arrived in another. In the second, spatially I am still where I was at the beginning

 ॐ शान्ति-प्रदाय नमः Salutations to the giver of peace.
Keep smiling, as there is no occasion which is ever tragic to a student of Vedānta. From the higher standpoint, all activities around us are but the play of our own mind. Realize this Truth, and be at peace with yourself.

The easiest way to make another one smile at you is to smile at him first. So it is with peace.

of the travel; there is no movement except in my consciousness," replied Anveshak thoughtfully and slowly.

"You are in a relatively higher state of meditation when the mind is quiet, and when it wanders, you are at a different level," the professor said.

Anveshak wanted to know what this higher state of the mind felt like. The professor offered Gurudev's words:

Our thoughts flow so continuously that there is no space between them. But concentrate upon the moment when one thought disturbance has ended and another thought disturbance has not started. If you can force your attention between these two thoughts, you see behind the mind, for the mind is nothing but thought flow. And if you can look through and between two successive thoughts, you must be face to face with the Lord.

"Isn't thinking about the Lord a thought too?" asked Anveshak.

"If you turn your complete attention upon Him, you are where there is no thought disturbance," answered Professor Vidyadhar.

ॐ जगत्साक्षिणे नमः: Salutations to the witness of the universe.

He, as the Infinite, is but a witness of the finite, inasmuch as the Self is an uninterested Illuminator of what is happening in the harem of the intellect, in the arena of the mind, in the courtyard of the body, and in the wide expanse of the world without.

In the quiet moments of contemplation, remain as a disinterested witness of all thoughts that parade in front of you.

Both sat in companionable silence, enjoying the cool morning air and the chirping of birds. Then Professor Vidyadhar spoke:

Detach yourself from the body-mind-intellect equipment and its field of activity in objects-emotions-thoughts and attach yourself to the Higher.

Anveshak looked at him quizzically.

"Those were the words of Gurudev, when he was asked what the initial step for meditation was," the professor said.

By this time, the yoginī had opened her eyes and spotted both of them. They stood chatting for a bit, when Anveshak announced that he was going to meditate.

"When you look at your bed, what do you think about?" was the yoginī's abrupt response.

"Sleep," he said, knowing this was going somewhere.

"The same way, set up a place which you think of as your seat of meditation."

"You don't seem to do that, I have seen you practice in different places," he challenged.

The professor said, "Damayanti has been practicing for some years

---

Reflection : Swami Siddhananda

Gurudev used to tell us that whatever project you undertake, treat it as a sādhanā. Taking care of elderly parents and children is the householder's sādhanā. For children, study is their sādhanā. To disciples he used to say taking care of devotees and the Chinmaya center is their sādhanā. Gurudev used to tell us all the time to do our personal sādhanā. In 1974 at an occasion in Mumbai, Gurudev told me: "It took thirty years of sādhanā for me not to talk bad about others."

now. You are a beginner, and Gurudev has said the same thing that she just suggested:

> After you set up your prayer room or your private chapel or a corner where you want to meditate, try to use the same place every day. Don't change it; use the same seat, the same place — because slowly that corner, that seat, gathers an atmosphere of its own. It becomes a psychological and spiritual harbor. By association of ideas, the moment you sit there, your mind automatically becomes quiet."

After throwing an apologetic look at the yoginī, Anveshak headed home with some trepidation. Was he capable of focusing? Could he really do this?

A few hours later, he felt ready to sit by the altar in his small pūjā room. As he sat in the quiet surroundings, while his body held still, the sounds of his inhalations and exhalations began to distract him. He adjusted his body to lessen the sound. As he sat with his eyes closed, he remembered Gurudev's words: Controlling the breath would allow control of all the functions of the body, such as the circulatory, excretory, sensory, digestive, and thought systems. If they functioned smoothly, the body and mind would be in a state of controlled rest.

Anveshak focused his attention completely on his breathing. He consciously slowed it and created a rhythm for himself. He found it restful. Was this meditation? He continued this for some weeks

ॐ सन्तुष्टाय नमः: Salutations to the ever-contented one.

Once or twice a day, a seeker should struggle hard to bring the mind into perfect quietude. The rest of the time, even while experiencing the various phenomena of the outer world, he should cultivate the habit of turning the mind into inner quietude. Continuously live this. This is the fulfillment of all spiritual practices!

The experience of deep inner quietude will express itself as contentment, causeless joy, alertness, and unconditional compassion.

when he recalled the professor telling him to attach himself to the Higher. How?

He went to the professor one day. Vidyadhar repeated the story of how Gurudev, when he was a young boy was asked by his aunt to sit through elaborate pūjās every day. To entertain himself, he would stare at the pictures of the gods in front of him. He particularly liked the visual of Lord Śiva with the smiling eyes and beaming mouth. While he waited for the pūjā to end, he would play a game. He would look at the picture of Lord Śiva, then quickly close his eyes and would see the Lord exactly as he was in the picture.

"He had absorbed Lord Śiva's likeness into him?" asked Anveshak.

"So much, that Gurudev was able to call up his Lord whenever he wanted! Inside!" exclaimed the professor putting his hand on his heart.

Anveshak resolved to try this. It was not easy. His thoughts veered this way and that. Sometimes he would bring his thoughts back forcefully and at other times cajole them to stay put at the feet of his Lord.

He went to Yoginī Damayanti. "At the risk of being repetitive," she said deciding to have some fun, "engage in repetition."

Anveshak harked back to what she had mentioned to him weeks ago. He had been so caught up in understanding the nature of the mind, he had not done what she had asked him to do. So, instead of taking her bait, he just said, "japa."

"Do you love your mother more or mine?"

"Mine," he said a bit hesitantly not wanting to offend her.

ॐ ईश्वराय नमः Salutations to the Lord, the ruler.

He resides in all living beings as Life; in His presence matter becomes vibrant and dynamic, capable of perceiving, feeling, and thinking.

The Lord resides in all: sinner or saint — all are worthy of respect. Shun none!

"You have never met my mother or thought of her, so how could you love her? The more you think of something or someone, the more attached you get to the object of your thought."

Anveshak understood that logic. Damayanti asked again, "What do you see in your mind's eye when I say 'Shanti Sevadas'?"

Thinking of the doctor's gentle wife brought a spontaneous smile on Anveshak's face, "Shantiji in prayer."

"The same way when you repeat your Lord's name, you will see Him. Isn't that what you are trying to do? Japa will give you single-pointed focus," the yoginī said.

Over the following weeks, Anveshak diligently practiced japa. The professor sent him details about how Gurudev had said the 108 beads on the japamala should be rotated on the fingers, and Anveshak followed the guidelines. He found it hard initially to concentrate and complete one round of 108 beads. Slowly and steadily though, as his anxiety subsided and he focused more on the chanting with absolute attention than getting to a count of 108, his thoughts were

ॐ प्रसन्नात्मने नमः Salutations to the ever-cheerful one.

The perfected man, living absorbed in the Self, equally disseminates joyous perfection, cheer, and bliss to all, at all times. It depends on the equipment that approaches him to take a greater or lesser share of it.

There is nothing of this world that can really upset your cheerful mind, unless you allow it to happen.

steady like the flow of milk on the Śivalinga. He would at times be able to do only 20 or 30 counts on the japa mala beads, but could find deep silence after completing his japa. His concentration improved, and he found joy in feeling closer to the Lord. But difficulties remained.

"I am very annoyed when I get up from the meditation seat," he confessed to the professor one day as they finished their morning jog together.

"At whom?"

"Myself and everything else," said Anveshak feeling irked at the very thought. "Am I not supposed to feel more peaceful?"

"Don't get frustrated, Anveshak," cautioned the professor. "Do you feel sleepy when you are seated?"

"Yes. What should I do?" asked Anveshak almost plaintively. The Professor quoted Gurudev:

> The seekers, during their early practices, should not overindulge in the world of their perceptions nor try to practice overly long and weary hours of meditation and force their inner silence.

The professor continued, "Economize your energy, Anveshak, and don't overdo it. And, at all times, keep your mind cheerful. Smile, not just with your lips, but truly smile with your entire being. You will find yourself under less pressure and will have fewer irritations. Gurudev has said that a serene mind is the most effective instrument for contemplation."

Sādhanā

- Exercise diligence in your practice.
- Persevere.
- Adopt a joyful mind.

XVII

Integrating Head and Heart: Governing the Inner World

There was Lord Kṛṣṇa! Blue form! Smiling! Flute in hand! Feet crossed! Anveshak was overjoyed. "Śrī Kṛṣṇa Sharanam Mama." His eyes flew open. He had been able to conjure the image of the Lord with crystal-like clarity while chanting His name. Finally. For a while now, he had been doing what Gurudev had instructed, which was to drown the usual thoughts from the outside world with loud chanting. On some days, he had been tempted to yell the name of the Lord out aloud with his mouth when he found the distractions too much. But with practice and devotion he had learned to do the loud chanting mentally, when he caught his thoughts swerving away from the Lord. But today — he felt success seeing Kṛṣṇa's image appear in his mind!

Anveshak was tempted to restart the exercise and experience the mental vision again. Then he remembered the caution about conserving energy. He also remembered what Gurudev had said: the goal was not to lengthen the mood of quietude but to keep practicing so that the depth of the silence would increase. So after prostrating to the Lord on his altar, he got ready to go to work at Dr. Sevadas's office.

But before leaving he called the professor to tell him about his auspicious experience. He was taken aback when the professor quoted Gurudev:

> To quieten the mind and bring it exclusively to the piece of job in your hand is a knack, not an achievement or a great art. Some people have it, but some others have to develop it. One who has integrated the mind and intellect is sure to succeed, whether he is functioning in the outer world or the spiritual path.

Vowing to himself that he would have the professor explain what that meant, Anveshak set off happily to work. After having spent an eventful day during which he spontaneously spread cheer all around, he went to Professor Vidyadhar's office on the university campus.

"Well, you have obviously been able to develop some single-pointedness, but it is complete only when your japa continues even while your sense organs are interacting with the outer world," the professor said on being queried by Anveshak about his morning phone call.

"I shouldn't talk or hear anything except what's related to the Lord?"

The professor replied with a question, "What happens after you have listened to a whole album of music? Which song do you hum?"

ॐ निजानन्दाय नमः **Salutations to the one happy with himself.**

When an individual's mind has been arrested from its agitated roaming in the world and fixed consistently upon the Self, by degrees, the mind gathers more and more quietude, and ultimately, when the flow of thoughts ceases, the mind also ends. When the mind has ended, the individual is awakened to the experience of the infinite nature of the Self. Naturally, the meditator comes to revel in supreme Bliss.

The bliss of the Self is not related to any object, thought, or experience. Therefore, it cannot be initiated by any act of self-will.

Without having to ruminate too much over it, Anveshak said, "The last one."

"Exactly, and isn't that the one that runs through your head the entire time till you hear another piece of music? You have to give your mind the job of chanting while you go about your daily interactions. That chant should be firmly rooted in your subconscious, so no matter what else you are hearing or seeing, that chant or mantra is continuously playing in the background," he said. "It is unlike other habits that pop up due to external triggers. Japa should continue without any external aid."

This was not difficult for Anveshak. In fact, while filing papers at the office, he had realized he was silently chanting. It had not been something conscious but it had happened automatically. He mentioned it to the professor.

ॐ सत्यसंकल्पाय नमः Salutations to the one with conviction.
The scriptures declare that not only is Truth the goal, and Truthfulness the path, but that very path is laid out with 'slabs' of Truthfulness. A consistent way of living, cemented by the values of intellectual truthfulness, widens the path and makes life an easy freeway to spiritual success.

Determine to live with intellectual honesty — confirm your convictions through consistent practice.

Professor Vidyadhar nodded and said, "When that happens, you have destroyed a thought that would have arisen and have supplanted it with your japa. In the process you are creating new and positive vāsanās."

"Am I adding to my vāsanā overload?" Then Anveshak grasped it, "Or are my old vāsanās getting replaced by better ones?"

"You are creating vāsanās, with the help of which your mind will come more and more under your sway," the professor said.

Just then there was a knock on the door. The professor opened it to let in yoginī Damayanti, who had come to borrow some books from him. When the two men assured her she was not interrupting and was welcome to join in, she too made herself comfortable on the chair by the window and listened to them recount what had transpired till then.

Anveshak asked, "What does Gurudev mean when he says that an integrated mind and intellect will lead to success? "Aren't the mind and the intellect the same? Aren't both composed of thoughts?"

"Yes, both are thoughts, but the nature of thoughts determines whether it is the mind or intellect," the Professor clarified and added, "When feelings and emotions keep changing and shifting, it is the mind and when there is determination and focus it is the intellect, according to Gurudev."

"Is feeling a thought, too?"

ॐ निरुपमाय नमः Salutations to the incomparable one.

The outer mind facing the objects of the world is called the objective mind (manas), and the inner mind is called the subjective mind (buddhi). That individual is unique in whom the objective and subjective aspects of the mind work in union with each other, and in moments of doubt, the objective mind readily comes under the disciplining influence of the subjective mind. Unfortunately, except for a rare few, the majority of us have minds that are split.

An outstanding person stands above the rest by not allowing tumultuous thoughts in the mind to overpower the intellect.

"Every experience is known to us only as thought. That is why Gurudev while explaining his famous BMI chart said, with the mind you are a feeler of emotions and with the intellect you are a thinker of thoughts!" said the Professor.

The yoginī chuckled."If they are not integrated — you're looking at the unhappiest couple ever," she declared.

As the professor grinned, Anveshak, now confused, asked, "Who?"

"When you were on the bridge, were you reasonable or emotional?" asked the yoginī in her usual roundabout way.

"Emotional."

"What happened to reason?"

"Hummmm…."

"Yes, hummmm. Your intellect had just been divorced by your mind."

"What happened when the doctor talked to you that day?"

"Reason returned."

"Mind and intellect got married again," pronounced the yoginī.

"The doctor was the marriage counselor," said Anveshak softly.

The professor said, "A good one at that. But in the quest that you are on, you are your only counselor, your only friend. Only you can bring the mind and intellect together.

ॐ ज्ञानयोगिने नमः Salutations to the jñāna-yogī.

When desires are not murmuring, thoughts cannot arise; and when thoughts do not rise, there will be complete cessation of action. When an individual, through study, satsaṅga, and intelligent thinking, has come to observe life and its happenings with the right attitude and intellectual poise, he automatically gets established in Yoga.

Yoga is not a mere physical posture; it is a mental poise achieved through intellectual clarity and calmness of mind.

"You mean detach from stuff around you. Remove nascent desires. Love the Lord. Negate your vāsanās. And only I can do this. Am I summing it up so far? " asked Anveshak.

The professor nodded. After some moments of silence, Anveshak asked, "What is desire, by the way?"

"It is the mind's projection of happiness on any object or person, said Professor Vidyadhar and continued, "When you entertain such a notion and you happen to get the object in question, the mind suddenly becomes quiet, feeling accomplished. This is the temporary joy you feel."

"And I feel unhappy when I don't get the desire satisfied!" Anveshak exulted in his understanding. He realized the cause for the pain that he had been experiencing was due to his 'failure' in love. But now he knew, love did not fail — desire had failed!

"Yes. Remember desires are what make the mind and intellect incompatible and creates disharmony in the marriage," said Professor Vidyadhar.

"What happens when a husband tells the wife that he is in the office and instead is actually at a bar with his friends?" asked the yoginī.

"His lie creates friction," replied Anveshak.

"We should strive to live truthfully. Our mind, intellect, and action should all be in accord," said the yoginī.

ॐ शुद्धसत्त्वाय नमः: **Salutations to the pure-hearted one.**

None of the activities of the body-mind-intellect equipment can ever bring about any contamination upon the immaculate Reality, the Self, even though It lends Its Existence and Energy to the whirls of matter around it. It Itself is never involved in the imperfect panting of the inert matter-conditionings.

A lotus stays untouched by the water on which it lives. So, too, does the Guru in the world. Hence, the Guru's feet are often extolled as Lotus Feet!

"This is also ahiṁsā — non-violence within yourself," said Professor Vidyadhar and quoted Gurudev in support of what the yoginī had said:

Satyam, or truthfulness, is the means to govern our inner world of mind and intellect. The outer world is a great university providing us with innumerable opportunities from which to learn. When these experiences have been well churned in our mind and the intellect has come to a firm decision, we must have the honesty and conviction to act upon it...Truthfulness enjoins us to live according to our intellectual convictions. We all have ideals, but we often fall prey to our senses and compromise with them. This is dishonest living.

Anveshak heard this with great attention. He summed up again, "Self-control for the body, ahiṁsā at the mental level, and truthfulness in action..."

The professor completed the thought, "Gurudev said these were the three great principles on which the edifice of life stands."

As the room went silent with each absorbed in his or her thoughts, the yoginī suddenly asked, "What separates the human species from the four-legged ones on earth?"

"Intellect," said Professor Vidyadhar as both of them looked pointedly at Anveshak.

"What?" asked Anveshak as though he had been attacked.

"What do you plan to do with yours?" asked the yoginī.

"Am I not using it?" asked Anveshak.

"Well, you are going to practice getting it in harmony with your mind. After that, what are you going to do with it?"

Still at a loss, Anveshak was silent. The professor filled in the gap, "Continue contemplation."

"I have to first see how to live in harmony within and without. I know you will both help me understand when I am ready," said Anveshak.

Sādhanā

- Control emotions.
- Use reason.
- Integrate conviction and action.

XVIII

Contemplation: Zeroing In

The Lord was not only someone he came to know in ritualized worship, but now was also a constant in Anveshak's mind and on his lips. The Lord was the first thought when he woke up each morning and the last when he went to bed. On some days he just bubbled with joy. There were times he felt a serenity he could not describe. And yet...

There were days when incidents at work or memories from his childhood would randomly pop up, and by association of thoughts, it would feel like a dam had burst in his increasingly sensitive mind. Both the yoginī and the professor had told him that this was definitely going to happen, and what he needed to do was to be ever vigilant and bring the mind back to where he wanted it to be.

And there were other times when he was inundated with the experiences from his past. Something that had been said to him by people he had considered his friends would disturb him. Hurt, he would spring up from his seat of meditation and go for a jog to clear his head with physical activity. To steady himself he would repeat, "My life is led by His will. His will, will be done!"

One morning, he jogged to the park where he knew the yoginī would be meditating and the professor would pass by while doing his daily run.

"Gurudev has said to forgive. Look within yourself and find compassion, Anveshak," the professor said kindly. His jog over, he stood looking at Anveshak with empathy.

"I thought about it, professor. Ahiṁsā includes forgiveness. When I realize that the happenings in my life are not the result of anyone's pre-meditated plan, I am able to let go easily," Anveshak replied.

"Wonderful! The scriptures tell us to forgive all is to love all," Professor Vidyadhar said.

"Forgiving is not enough?"

"It wasn't enough for Meera, was it? She loved her Lord Kṛṣṇa but she was always restless and in agony, longing for a vision of her beloved Kṛṣṇa all the time!"

"Well, she was insecure, not knowing where He was," replied Anveshak. He remembered a discourse that he had attended about the great saint Meerabai who had given up everything for her beloved Lord. At that time, he had interpreted it as Meera not being happy with her life's situation and seeking some solace in God.

"That fear, the desire to be loved, is in you too," said the professor.

He was right, thought Anveshak. He was dependent on others for his happiness. But he couldn't even depend on the Lord. Even Meera suffered from being dependent. What then?

"Yourself!" cried Professor Vidyadhar."You are sat-cit-ānanda!"

"Huh?"

"You are bliss itself!" the professor continued in an excited voice.

"Right," said Anveshak, his old cynical habit peeping through.

ॐ पुरुषोत्तमाय नमः Salutations to the best among men.

Vedānta calls upon man to rediscover himself to be nothing short of God Himself. And when a mortal has fully realized and comes to live continuously the God-consciousness, no sorrows can approach him. Such a rare one alone is best among all.

"God made us," say the faithful. "We created God," scream the faithless. "God is your essence," reminds Vedānta!

The professor looked deflated."Contemplate on that," he commanded.

"Huhh?" went the bewildered Anveshak.

The professor slowed down."What are you seeking with all your efforts?" he asked.

Anveshak did not reply. Many answers came to him: silence, peace, happiness. He knew instinctively that it was not what the professor was asking him.

The professor took another approach."Do you know the difference between seeking and searching?"

Really! Was he in for a language lesson now? Anveshak shook his head carefully.

"Gurudev has said we seek something we don't know, like all those planets we seek to discover by sending out spacecrafts and orbiters. Searching is to look for something we know is there but cannot get to immediately," the professor lectured.

"The point being?" asked Anveshak politely.

"Are you alive?" asked the yoginī who had joined them by now.

"Huhhh?" It was Anveshak's favored response today.

"You know you are alive because you are breathing," she went on briskly, "but what makes you live?"

"What is life?" added Professor Vidyadhar.

Anveshak stood perplexed as he was bombarded with thought-provoking questions from both sides.

ॐ विभवे नमः **Salutations to the all-pervading one.**

He who has discovered that the Self within himself is none other than the all-pervading Consciousness, which is nondual, he instantaneously discovers It to be in the core of all pluralistic forms around him.

Beyond the names and forms of the world is the underlying Essence.
It is within you, yet without you!

The professor used Gurudev's words to explain what he meant:

> This silent and mysterious power called Life expresses itself
> through every one of us, and, because of Life, we are what we are.
> Minus this mysterious power, you and I are mere zeros — mere
> bundles of manure. This great mighty presence enlivens all living
> beings — plant, animal and human — we are all manifestations of
> this mighty power.

When the professor paused, Anveshak carefully asked, "What is the connection between this power called Life and the God that I worship?"

The Professor smiled and said, "That is for you to contemplate. In contemplation, the goal is to move toward that power, slowly and gradually, and eventually, if there is sincerity, reach it," said the professor almost to himself. "We know it's there; we just have to get to it."

"In Vaikuṇṭha?" asked Anveshak, ever the bhakta.

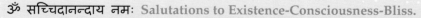

ॐ सच्चिदानन्दाय नमः Salutations to Existence-Consciousness-Bliss.

Though the supreme Truth is independent of the world of matter, in stone life, It exhibits Itself as Existence; in plant life, as being Conscious of its own Existence; and in animals, as being Conscious of emotions and feelings as well. Both animals and human beings pursue happiness, but only humans seek eternal happiness. Religion and spirituality are for the human being alone.

Contemplate thus: "I Exist; I am Aware of my Existence; I am Aware that I am Blissful Existence."

Professor Vidyadhar shook his head, still immersed in his own thoughts about the Enlivener of Life.

"Kailash?" asked Anveshak.

"In yourself," came the same reply he had received minutes ago.

Anveshak touched his heart and raised an eyebrow in query.

The Professor shook his head. Anveshak touched his head and got the same head shake.

The yoginī was watching this silent exchange."Goodness! Life is not a mysterious person sitting somewhere. The Spark of Existence is in you and in me and everyone. We are all alive, aren't we?" she said throwing her arms around expansively.

"Is this power, this spark you are referring to, God?" asked Anveshak completing the question he had wanted to ask.

Vidyadhar highlighted the words which Gurudev had once used to explain God to a disbelieving young man:

> That which you now speak of as God, my boy, the Muslim calls Allah, the Christian refers to as 'My Father in Heaven,' the Parsi as Ahura Mazda. These are a few of the different ways in which HE or IT is referred to, but all are referring to the same supreme Principle. The Cause behind all causes, the Source of all that was, now is, and ever will be. The Vedas refer to it as Brahman, the Absolute, the Infinite.

ॐ तीर्थस्वरूपाय नमः **Salutations to the one of holy nature.**

In meditation, there is a hazy period of awareness, wherein we are conscious of ourselves nearing the Transcendental; that state of samādhi where there is still a vestige of the ego is called savikalpa samādhi. The egoless moment when a Yogi experiences the infinite Bliss of pure Existence is called nirvikalpa samādhi. That is the experience of Godhood, the Iśvara darśana. After that, there is no falling back into impulses of the lower, worldly life anymore.

The vision of God is the most sacred accomplishment in human life. One who has this vision has reached the destination — destiny no more affects him!

"So if God is in me and you, why am I rushing to the temple and praying to the deities?" Anveshak demanded. He, like Shantiji, had fallen in love with Lord Kṛṣṇa and it was inconceivable to him that it was pointless for him to have devoted himself to something that was not. Were these people leading him up the garden path and misdirecting him? He felt a flicker of distrust.

"When you go on vacation, don't you take pictures of the things you see, the food you eat and the places where you stay? Isn't that how you remember the trip? In the same way, you worship your Lord to remember the Supreme," said the Professor.

"It's important to remember that what you worship is the manifestation of the Supreme, not the Supreme itself," added the yoginī.

Anveshak was pacified, yet not convinced."When I am in the seat of meditation I am focused on the likeness of the Lord. Is there something else I should be doing?"

The professor thought for a while. "Gurudev, while lecturing on the *Bhagavad-gītā*, talked about how we could contemplate on an aspect of the nature of the Absolute: Omniscient, Primordial, Controller, Smallest, Sustainer, Indescribable, Resplendent, and Transcendental."

Their whole conversation was punctuated with long silences.

Breaking the stillness, the yoginī asked, "What happens when you use the intellect to meditate on all these aspects of the nature of the Absolute?"

ॐ परमाय नमः Salutations to the Supreme.

The uncaused Cause for the entire world of phenomena is the supreme Self, which, though residing in everyone and thrilling the inert matterfield around each embodied creature into the play of life, does not in Itself and by Itself act, just like space that allows everything to remain in it, yet nothing can contaminate it. The Supreme is subtler than space.

A boat should be in the water but not water inside the boat! Be in the world, but don't allow the world to occupy you!

"These are abstract terms. How can I think about them? At best, I would think about the meaning…but without any focus!" cried out Anveshak.

"You need to get beyond the intellect," said Vidyadhar. "Your thinking will stop, and wonder will begin when you know that all these terms are indicating that One which operates in each of us as Life itself!"

"What does that feel like?" asked the yoginī curiously.

"If I explain what a magnolia's scent is, you might understand it. If I compare it to an experience you might have had with the scent of something else, you might understand it better. But to know the scent and enjoy it to its fullest, you have to experience it yourself. You will have no reason to compare it with anything else. That was Lord Kṛṣṇa's answer to Arjuna in the *Gītā* when Arjuna asked what that State beyond the intellect would be like," said Vidyadhar.

"I already know more happiness now than I have ever felt in my life, including when I had wealth and success," pondered Anveshak aloud, "I can only imagine what this State must be like."

Reflection: Acharya Vilasini Balakrishnan

Pūjya Gurudev in a letter wrote to me: Be regular in study and meditation. Don't judge its qualities. Hosepipe everyone around you with your love.

ॐ संन्यासिने नमः Salutations to the great renunciate.

Our intellect can register a situation or a condition only with reference to the comparative estimate of its opposite. Thus, I can understand light only with reference to my knowledge of darkness. If comparison and contrast are the methods of knowing for the mind-intellect instruments, a renunciate who has risen above the dualities is one who has transcended these instruments.

The mind of a renunciate is like that of the moon in broad daylight. Its light is there, yet not there!

Vidyadhar looked at Anveshak and told him what Gurudev had said:

> Even if you have quietened the mind two percent, then you experience two percent of Him. If the mind is quietened one hundred percent, you can experience Him one hundred percent. This peace, you become fascinated by it, you become more addicted to meditation — because, my friends, why are you struggling outside after all, physically, mentally and intellectually? So that you may be happy, is it not? What you need is not money but happiness. When you realize that there is a subtler happiness — a larger dose of happiness available within yourself without all the paraphernalia of the world of objects and their accessories — don't you think you will start holding onto it more and more?

"Enjoy the Joy in your own self," said the yoginī.

"Enjoy the journey itself!" exclaimed Anveshak.

Sādhanā

- Travel from happiness to peace.
- Understand the nature of the Divine.

Forgiveness is a mental balm to heal all mental ulcers.

Jñāna Yoga

Life Divine

PLAIN TRUTH

XIX

Knowledge: The Torchlight

Anveshak was determined to find the Spark of Life.

Ruminating on this, he went to Vidyadhar's office one evening, where the professor sat behind a cluttered desk grading papers, but was more than happy to have Anveshak visit. Smiling, he asked, "What brings you here at this hour?"

Always one to say without hesitation what was on his mind, Anveshak articulated what he wanted and followed it up with, "What do I need to do?"

"Gain spiritual knowledge."

"How?"

"Become a student of Vedānta. Study the Upaniṣads."

Anveshak did not know the meaning of the two Sanskrit words and said so.

"The knowledge we seek," said Vidyadhar, "is compiled in four books known as the Vedas, each of which is divided into four sections. That section of each Veda, which contains the greatest philosophical truths, is known as the Upaniṣad."

Anveshak repeated, "Upa-ni-shad."

"Yes, Gurudev says the word Upaniṣad means 'sit-down-near.' The Upaniṣad is taught to those who approach a Master in humility and practice the philosophy of life with his guidance to attain liberation. Just as music or dance cannot be learned by reading a book, the great secret of happiness can also not be learned by just reading books."

Anveshak nodded as the professor continued, "The study of this, is known as Vedānta, a Sanskrit word that means 'the end of all knowledge' — the ultimate Knowledge."

"Who wrote these books?"

"No one."

Anveshak flopped down on the chair in front of Vidyadhar's desk and looked up at the ceiling of the professor's office. Really, this was too much. Books without authors! Could there be honey without bees, or butterflies without caterpillars?

An amused Vidyadhar continued, "The ultimate Truth is a revelation. The Masters transmitted the ultimate Knowledge orally to their sincere students. The students 'sat-near' and learned from their Master."

"But who were these Masters who contemplated the Truth?" asked Anveshak.

"Sages who lived thousands of years ago," said the professor.

"No names?"

"Some names have come down to us, but as Gurudev has explained, these Masters were great seekers who were not interested in creating

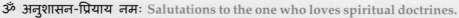

 ॐ अनुशासन-प्रियाय नमः Salutations to the one who loves spiritual doctrines.
An honest and sincere effort on the part of the seeker is absolutely necessary if the words indicating the Truth are to be correctly interpreted, understood, and efficiently made use of. To him who devotedly approaches the scriptures, Truth will reveal itself.

Do not approach scriptures as a scholar; see them through the loving eyes of the saints!

their own legacies and instead rose above their own individualities in finding the greatest Truth. In that Truth lies the permanent happiness you are now looking for," said the professor.

"How did the revelations become the four Vedas?" asked Anveshak.

"It was the great Sage Vyasa who gathered the oral knowledge and compiled it into books. We know him today as Veda Vyasa," said the professor. An erudite man whose work revolved around research and writing, Professor Vidyadhar became silent, momentarily overcome by the enormity of what one Master had done for humankind.

"If these books are so profound and Vedānta is a philosophy that shows the way to inner fulfillment and happiness, why don't more people know of it? No one talks about it in my bhajan group or when I am at the temple," Anveshak said.

"Gurudev agreed with what you are saying and lamented that the beauty of Upaniṣadic teachings had been hidden in the 'overgrowth' and '1,001 interpretations' of these scriptures. Here's how he explained it:"

A true religion has two important limbs: the ritualistic injunctions and the philosophical support. Most of us generally accept the former as religion. But the rituals and formalities are mere superstitions without philosophy; philosophy reinforces the external practices of the formalities and blesses them with a purpose and an aim. Even so, philosophy without any actual practice is madness. Ritual and reason must go hand in hand.

"Where can I find these books?" asked Anveshak.

Vidyadhar stood up, browsed through his bookshelves, and placed a stack of books on his desk. "Many Upaniṣads were compiled, but time has left us only 108. Of these, ten are the most significant, and Gurudev has written brilliant commentaries on eight of them, in

line with the teachings of Ādi Śaṅkarācārya. He has written his commentaries in the style of a modern thinker so that we can understand them readily."

"Ādi...?"

"The revered Saint Ādi Śaṅkarācārya was one of the greatest Vedāntic teachers and a reformist of the 8th century C.E. He pioneered the writing of commentaries on the Upaniṣads. Gurudev closely followed these teachings in all his writing and public lectures."

"I should start reading," said Anveshak, standing up and eyeing the pile on the desk.

The professor chuckled gently. "Anvashek, these are not to be read like a news magazine, from which you get some facts and feel informed. Gurudev used to say that we should not run through the scriptures, the scriptures should run through us!"

"I should understand them completely?" asked Anveshak as he sat down again.

ॐ कृतात्मने नमः Salutations to the Self-realized one.

A Guru must be perfect in all his conduct; there is no excuse for him to be vulgar in any aspect of his living.

Discipline defines a disciple; the same discipline exemplified should be the Guru.

"Vedānta emphasizes personal experience more than most other schools of philosophy. The Masters, or ṛsis, as we call them, found what they were looking for through their own experience. If someone were to tell you that in winter the beaches of Los Angeles were better than those in Oregon, and provided evidence with temperatures and pictures, you may have learned something new, but unless you yourself were to experience it, the experience would still not be yours, but remain another person's."

"My reading about their experience will not help?"

"Reading alone will not. Gurudev provided a good example. He said, 'Your painting might be exactly like a photograph, but unless you have grasped the essence of what you are painting and are able to express it, you will only be a craftsman and not an artist.'"

"What am I to do?" asked a perplexed Anveshak.

ॐ तपोवनशिष्याय नमः Salutations to the disciple of Swami Tapovanam.

We, Swami Tapovanam's disciple family, have to see that he finds an ample field for him to express himself. It is not sufficient that we evolve only in study — we must learn to realize Him in visible expression everywhere. It is a glorious chance now to take a sacred oath that we shall not rest contented until he is fulfilled. Let us observe the Pūrṇimā (full moon) day of every month as a day for inspiration and self-dedication.

Guru is the compassionate expression of the dispassionate Self. He teaches through dispassion how to renounce the world and through compassion how to love God.

"The path of knowledge is not for the faint-hearted. Gurudev said:"

> A seeker in Vedānta is expected to carry out daring intellectual flights to the Unknown through a process of deep study, vigorous reflections, and tireless meditations … it must necessarily mean that he should have a special quality of the head and heart.

"Read, reflect, contemplate, and make it my own," Anveshak iterated what he had heard.

Vidyadhar said, "Most people go astray for want of conviction." He continued to quote:

> We have faith, but not firm conviction. We have certainty, but not self-resurrecting, adamantine belief. Those dynamic convictions that drive us to spectacular actions and blazing results cannot be had by accident. They are not built-in resources in any individual. We have to discover and cultivate them in ourselves, by our own study and planned self-education.

Anveshak thought over Gurudev's words. "Will the study of the scriptures help firm up my desire to learn, or maybe it will challenge me too much and dishearten me?"

"Ah! Gurudev anticipated that, and therefore urged us to develop 'adamantine belief.' The deep study of the Upaniṣads and the *Bhagavad-gītā* will help rearrange your thoughts, provide a proper vision of life, and solidify your goal. But life happens."

ॐ पावनाय नमः **Salutations to the holy one.**

According to Upaniṣadic lore, in the 'cave of the heart' is the seat of the intellect, and the saints continue to explain that in the 'cave of the intellect' is the seat of the Self. When we are inside a cave, we all know that all around us is nothing but the rocks of the cave. Therefore, 'cave of the heart' must mean an atmosphere where one is surrounded by love, tenderness, compassion, and so on. He who lives in such a cave is Holy!

The cave of the heart is not for hiding; it is meant for abiding!

"You mean I could slide off?" asked Anveshak.

"I am sure there were times when you were in college when you decided not to do your assignments or skip class because you thought the lectures were boring. That could happen in your study of the scriptures.

You overcame boredom and other challenges in college, because you knew you would not get your degree otherwise. Now, on the spiritual path, there is no degree being awarded, and no one monitoring you. Is that going to be a challenge? Only you know the answer to that."

"I need to have fortitude and apply self-effort," said Anveshak softly.

"Here is what Gurudev said:"

Nārāyaṇa never gives you, gift-wrapped, what you desire. He gives you the seeds — the tendency, the faith in yourself for what you want to do. The more you do it, the more He gives you the faith. And by the power of faith in yourself and your goal, you win your desire.

"And if I don't understand what I read, what should I do?" Anveshak asked.

The professor turned and gazed at Gurudev's picture sitting on his desk and said, "You need someone who recognizes your seeking heart and guides you so that, in time, you will gradually be able to understand the scriptures by yourself."

"A teacher."

"A Guru," the professor corrected. The one who can sow, irrigate, and help grow the tree of faith in you. The Guru is the one who will sustain your interest by exemplifying what is said in the scriptures," said Vidyadhar, eyes fixed on Gurudev's picture.

As both of them sat lost in their thoughts, Anveshak slowly formulated his question, "How is this knowledge different from other knowledge that may give me permanent happiness?"

The professor stared at him, momentarily disoriented, as the question echoed the central query from the *Muṇḍakopaniṣad*, which Anveshak surely knew nothing of. He counter-questioned, "What does happiness mean?"

"Happiness! Everyone knows what that means," Anveshak replied quickly, not sure how to define it.

"When the orange tree in my yard blossoms and spreads its fragrance, it makes me happy; and when a student understands perfectly what I have taught, it makes me happy," said the professor.

Catching on, Anveshak said, "When I made money in the stock market, I was happy, and when I will get my new car, it will make me happy. I see a patient of Dr. Sevadas get better and I am happy. Helping Shantiji at the temple gives me happiness."

"You do see, don't you, that happiness means different things to each of us?"

Anveshak nodded.

"What gave you happiness earlier has now been replaced by your

 ॐ मेधाविने नमः: Salutations to the learned one.

 Power of memory, medhā, is not merely a prodigious capacity to memorize scriptures; it is the ability of the student listening to a Guru to at once be able to react intensely to his words and thus make the ideas explained his own at the very time of listening to them.

 Wisdom is to convert the knowledge into understanding by applying it instantly to oneself.

happiness in being a source of help to someone else. Your idea of happiness has changed with time," the professor pointed out.

Again, Anveshak nodded in agreement.

Vidyadhar continued, "The actions we engage in are with the outside world to satisfy our selfish desires. We are dependent on objects and people to make us happy. You will get your new car, but soon you will want a new model of the car. I may want more students to tell me that they like my class. When we don't get what we want, we are unhappy."

After thinking over on what he had heard, Anveshak understood that happiness, as he experienced it, was fleeting.

The professor now said, "Permanent happiness is freedom."

"Freedom from being dependent on others?" asked Anveshak.

"And freedom from the influence of outside objects and emotions, which now have the power to make us restless, ungrateful, and unhappy."

"I live in this world, and I have to interact with it," pointed out Anveshak.

"Of course! But Gurudev called it the 'art of right contact,' with people, objects, emotions, and thoughts," said the professor.

"Meaning?"

"Knowledge of right contact will change the way you view the world," said Vidyadhar.

ॐ सर्वहितचिन्तकाय नमः Salutations to the well-wisher of all.

Gurus must be well-meaning in the sense that they should not be mere gramophone records repeating what the scriptures say, but must be men so well-established in their own experience, and so familiar with the path, that they can interpret it to different types of students belonging to different climes and of different ages.

True service to others is to release others from self-created suffering caused by Self-forgetfulness.

"Will I still feel the need to drive a car?"

"You will still drive a car, but you may not desire an expensive car, whose only purpose is to bolster your vanity."

"My attitude toward material objects will change, which means my desires, thoughts and thinking will also change," said Anveshak. The professor looked pleased as he read aloud what Gurudev had said on reflection, or mananam:

> To do mananam, we need not renounce the world or run away into a quiet corner. It is most effectively undertaken by maintaining in one corner of the mind the thoughts related to what is learned from the Guru during śravaṇam — [and allowing those thoughts] to smolder. A small quantity of incense burning at one end of a hall can impart its fragrance throughout the hall, and even waft the same sweetness to the atmosphere outside the windows. So, too, the Vedāntic discourse heard once may be allowed to smolder at one end of the mind, and it will soon spread its fragrance into the wider world of one's own thoughts and ideas within, and speech and actions without.

"Since my thinking will not stop, where can the thoughts be redirected?" asked Anveshak.

"Toward discovering the bliss in you," said the professor.

The Spark of Life, thought Anveshak. The supreme Knowledge had to be gained.

Sādhanā

- Read the scriptures.
- Never waver.
- Have faith.
- Develop fortitude.
- Reflect.
- The Self is the seat of all happiness.

XX

Ego: The Colossal 'i'

The next few days at work were hectic. With the onset of the flu season, patients trooped in continuously, and Anveshak worked late into the evenings with Dr. Sevadas. Even as he unfailingly said his prayers and considered his meditation time sacrosanct, he was bursting with questions that had arisen in his mind as he read Gurudev's commentaries on the Upaniṣads, and was waiting to have them addressed by the professor.

His first chance came on the weekend as he waited in the park for Vidyadhar to finish his morning jog. The two found themselves on the same bench that they had sat on earlier many times, catching up or speaking on similar weighty matters.

Anveshak began with the basics. "Does this thing that enlivens all of us have a name?"

"The ṛṣis have called it Brahman, Truth, Consciousness," answered the professor.

"And is it like a power grid?"

"Yes. Just as the power grid lights up every home and street, Brahman lights up every individual," the professor said.

"And when the power grid fails, we die?"

"Can sugar stop being sweet?" the professor counter-questioned.

"It wouldn't be sugar then."

"Just as sweetness is the essential nature of sugar, the nature of the power grid, or Brahman, is deathlessness. It is eternal," said the professor.

"And yet I know I will die," said Anveshak.

"When the bulb in your living room lamp burns out, does the power supply to the lamp stop?" asked the professor, reverting to the earlier analogy.

"Obviously not," said Anveshak.

"You and I are like the bulb. Brahman is the power supply," said Vidyadhar.

Anveshak failed to understand. "Where is the power being supplied to if I am already dead?"

"Ah! But we don't die!" came the reply.

Anveshak felt his jaw drop when he heard the rather triumphant response from the professor. Was there some interstellar travel involved that he had no knowledge of? After long moments of silence and when the professor egged him on to speak, Anveshak said quietly, "I lit the pyre of my mother. She is dead. We will all die. This is not debatable."

ॐ धर्मसंस्थापकाय नमः: Salutations to the one who establishes dharma.

Dharma means not merely righteousness or goodness, but it indicates the essential nature of anything, without which it cannot retain its independent existence. Therefore, if we were to live as truly dynamic men in the world, we can do so only by being faithful to our true Nature. When the majority of the members of a community do not obey this great Truth, a great Master comes to present himself as the leader of men to revive the 'standard of life' and its moral values.

When the higher purpose of life is recognized, a Master is born! His mission becomes his life.

The professor said, "What dies is only the body."

"What else is there?"

"The expression of the eternal Brahman in you, known as the Ātman. The Ātman powers you. That is the true you," the professor said, recalling what Gurudev had said:

> The Truth-aspect in the individual, when it identifies with finite matter, comes to experience mortality. When this delusory identification has ended at the dawn of wisdom, the Self as the Self must necessarily attain the State of Immortality. The realm of the Self lies beyond the reach of death.

Anveshak got up from the park bench and began pacing, thinking furiously. The professor waited.

"This Ātman which I cannot see or feel or hear, according to you, is deathless. When we are cremated, it lives on; only the body burns. Have I understood it so far?"

"Perfect. If I were to ask you to describe yourself, what would you say?" asked the professor.

"I am single, of medium height, have black hair, and live in an apartment. I have several ideas on how businesses can be protected from failing. I have become more patient and sensitive to others, and I am striving to be permanently happy," was the reply.

"Notice how you mention physical attributes, emotional being and your thoughts?" asked the professor. "Gurudev said that's what we

> ॐ नित्याय नमः Salutations to the eternal one.
>
> The Self is present in all the states of experiences in all beings, and at all times. It is awake even while we are asleep, but we are not aware of this eternal Self in us, due to our preoccupations with the misapprehensions of the Reality.
>
> The one who sleeps does not know he is sleeping, and the One who knows never sleeps!

do, we identify with 'finite matter,' our body, mind and intellect, and believe that how we look and what we have and what we think or feel is who we are. Gurudev termed it 'fanciful stupidity.'"

Anveshak was taken aback. "Am I stupid? Are you saying none of it is relevant?"

"Not stupid… just deluded."

"Thank you," said Anveshak with exaggerated politeness.

Unfazed, the professor explained, "When we identify with matter, we create a monster called the ego."

"As a child, I was told ego meant arrogance and selfish individuality and that it should be tamped down," remarked Anveshak, as he sat down again on the bench.

The professor nodded his head, "For good reason. Ego is indeed a sense of individuality born of a deluded intellect which imagines, 'I am this powerful person' or 'I am the most popular' and then follows up with actions to support it."

From his bag, the professor got out a bar of chocolate and placed it on the space between them on the park bench and continued to speak, "Gurudev often illustrated his point with a food example. Right now, when you see the chocolate, your body might want to devour it, your mind from where the desire is emanating might be in agreement, but

---

ॐ परब्रह्मणे नमः: Salutations to the supreme Brahman.

All finite things end only to go back to the cause from which they were born. The Self is of the nature of Existence and therefore does not end. Thus, It has no cause into which It can go back; this also means that the Self, as such, is not the modification of anything. It is the ultimate Reality and hence has no beginning as well.

The gross body is mortal, while subtle and causal bodies transmigrate. What remains has no beginning and no end. Stay as That!

the intellect knows the calories and fat in there are not good for you, and the spiritual center is bemoaning your succumbing to the senses. Am I right?"

"Attachment to body and mind has created the ego, which has me at war with myself," groaned Anveshak.

The professor nodded, closed his eyes, and carefully repeated Gurudev's words from memory:

> In each of us there seems to be a multi-headed personality, each head demanding its own satisfaction and possessing its own tastes, standards, and values. Ordinary people attempt to gain a sense of complete happiness by acquiring, organizing, preserving, and playing with the sense objects of the world. However, as soon as one of the four personalities has found its happiness, the others revolt in dissatisfaction. Thus, the hydra-headed monster seeks happiness by drinking from a single cup, where there are four parched throats, each demanding a different beverage altogether.

In the silence that followed, Anveshak realized that it was not just the bar of chocolate that had him in conflict with himself. It was present in his relationships and even in simple things like how he wanted to spend his free time. And conflict, by its very nature, brought dissatisfaction and grief.

He complained, "I have four personalities — a severe case of multiple personality disorder. I may have to go to Dr. Sevadas!"

"Or fix the problem yourself."

When Anveshak raised his eyebrows, Vidyadhar reassured him

and said, "Your understanding of honesty, ahiṁsā, love for the Lord, and discipline in meditation are already smoothing your inner self and integrating it. With knowledge, the final step to the Spark of Life, as you call it, can be reached."

Touched by the encouraging words, Anveshak closed his eyes and sat silent for a few moments. Then he asked, "What should the identification be with if not the body, mind, or intellect?"

"The Ātman."

"Where is it?" cried a slightly annoyed Anveshak. That's what he was searching for, wasn't it?

"It is like an artichoke. To get to the center and enjoy its goodness, we have to peel off layers of leaves. Gurudev said the Ātman is veiled by layers of matter ranging from the gross to the subtle. The body is the grossest and we identify with it almost all the time," explained the professor.

"I am to identify with Ātman, which I cannot even perceive," sighed Anveshak.

"Ten years from now, will any of how you described yourself be relevant? There may be some grey hair on your head, your belly might have a bulge, your ideas may have changed, and you might be mentioning some other quality that has gained importance for you."

"Law of nature: things change," argued Anveshak.

ॐ भूम्ने नमः: **Salutations to the limitless one.**
The Self is described in the Upaniṣads as both the tiniest of the tiny and also as the biggest of the big. This means that the Self is an infinite, all-pervading Essence and that even the minutest space conceivable is pervaded by this great, divine Influence.

Infinity is that which is also in the finite, yet unconditioned by the finite. The teachings of Vedānta have an extensive effect on the seeker, much beyond the scope of religion.

"And with every change, the things that will make you happy will change, too. Yet you seek permanent happiness from these things!"

Anveshak was stumped. The professor took another tack, "The concept of who we are changes every moment. In childhood, youth, middle age, and old age, when we dream, when we are awake, there is a different concept of 'I' and yet, we are the same person. Agreed?"

Anveshak nodded. Of course he looked and sounded different at every stage, but he had been Anveshak through nursery, school, college, and down to the present.

"How do you know that you are the same person?" asked the professor.

"I am the same person!" exclaimed a surprised Anveshak.

"What's informing you of this?"

When Anveshak said nothing, the professor explained, "Gurudev said, 'If there is a set of continuous experiences, then there must be a changeless Factor in you which knows all changes.'"

In his mind's eye, Anveshak ran over his entire body, looking for what might have remained unchanged over the years. Nothing.

After giving him time, the professor asked, "Through the years in this birth alone, do you know what has remained changeless, Anveshak?" and without waiting for an answer, said, "That Spark of Life you are searching for, the Self, which expresses itself as 'I am.'"

ॐ श्रोत्रियाय नमः **Salutations to the one well-versed in scriptural knowledge.**

To guide and instruct a deluded soul and help him unwind himself and unravel the knotty traits in him, a teacher must, no doubt, have full realization, and he must also have a complete grasp of the great scriptures. Without this, even a Self-realized Master will not have the language or the technique of expression to convey his profound knowledge to his disciples.

Scriptures are like sculptures hidden in the stone; you will see their beauty when the Guru opens your eyes!

Changeless?

Anveshak asked, "Is it a bystander or a participant in my life?"

"It is a changeless observer unaffected by the joys and sorrows of the experiences of the ever-changing body and mind," said the professor.

"If it is always there, why can't I perceive it?" asked Anveshak.

"Because of the ego, we are so sure about ourselves. When we say definitively, 'I know,' 'I feel,' 'I think'; it is the ego that is saying it. We are so attached to the body, mind, and intellect that we don't even begin to look beyond."

Anveshak went quiet after this. It had been an information overload. There was much to think about.

Sādhanā

- Integrate thought and action.
- Let go.
- Increase knowledge of the Self.
- Reduce desires.
- Remind yourself that Ātman is changeless and deathless.

XXI

Māyā: The Illusionist

One Sunday afternoon, Anveshak sat by the pūjā altar in his home taking stock: Right knowledge would liberate him from his ego, that is, detach him from wrong notions about himself and attach him to the right one — the Self; right knowledge would redirect his mind so his thoughts would not be driven by desires and the ensuing actions and lead to the accumulation of more vāsanās; right knowledge would lead him to his inner bliss center. But how was this process to be monitored?

From all that he had heard so far, the locus of happiness was in him, had always been in him, and would always be in him. And yet, he had remained oblivious to its very existence. How was this possible?

Restless, he rose to his feet and moved toward the altar, seeking answers. No overwhelming insight arrived. Just then his phone rang and he saw it was yoginī Damayanti, who in her usual bright manner asked if he would like to join her and the professor for tea at the yoga studio. He agreed immediately. He had not met her in a while and her being a counterpoint to the seriousness of the professor meant there would be great conversation. He took along with him the book he had been reading.

As was often the case when the three of them were together, their informal meeting led to talk on matters of philosophy. Anveshak wanted to know about his ignorance.

"What about it?" asked Damayanti.

"I know the inner workings of my heart, kidney, and lungs; how come I don't know about the Ātman, or Brahman?"

"Went to the wrong school, did you?" teased the yoginī.

Smiling, the professor said, "It is Māyā."

"Who is Māyā?"

Damayanti let out a peal of laughter. Unoffended, Anveshak grinned.

"Māyā is not a mere mortal! No individual has that kind of influence," said the professor.

"Okay, what is Māyā?"

"The power that has the ability to delude," replied the professor.

"Where does the power come from?"

"From God. This power makes you see things that do not really exist and also veils those which do exist!"

"Why should God delude us?"

"Here is where you need to listen carefully," said Vidyadhar and continued, "According to Vedānta, God is not a person, though God is personified for easy comprehension."

"As Kṛṣṇa, Śiva, and so on?"

"Yes. God is essentially Brahman, and when we look from the standpoint of the world, Brahman is referred to as God, because ultimately Brahman is the origin of the entire creation, with the power of Māyā. Just like one is referred to as father only with respect to his son."

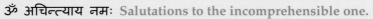

ॐ अचिन्त्याय नमः Salutations to the incomprehensible one.

He, as the Self, being the very life that energizes the mind and intellect, cannot be an object of their comprehension.

Turn within and stay as objectless Awareness!

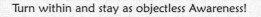

"So, why delusion?"

"When we don't see the world as Brahman and instead see the variety of names and forms, including our body, mind, and so on, we get caught in the quagmire of anger, lust, and various passions. Delusion is the result of confusion in thinking."

That startled Anveshak. He had imagined a 'Star Wars' kind of scenario, a good versus evil kind of thing happening in the cosmos somewhere, but here the good was creating trouble. "Brahman is in us as this ever-happy thing called Ātman — but he is in us by stealth, hiding?"

"Māyā, "Gurudev said, "is an indescribable, mighty, inscrutable power of God that causes you to forget your Self. This Self-forgetfulness is ignorance."

"But why does God deliberately create delusion?" asked a puzzled Anveshak.

"He doesn't, we create it out of our ignorance of the Self," Vidyadhar said and added, "Don't you suffer in your dream though it is your own creation? Why? The ancients thought crossing the ocean was a wonder. At this point in time we think intergalactic travel is a wonder. Gurudev pointed out that anything our intellect cannot comprehend we label as a 'wonder.' Similarly, Māyā is a wonder."

Anveshak was lost and said so.

"Well," said the professor, "what do you use to create and understand new ideas?"

"The intellect," said Anveshak.

"Which is what we are attached to and is the part of the apparatus that keeps us away from the Self, yes?"

"You are saying that the intellect cannot comprehend ignorance because ignorance has created the intellect?!" Anveshak sat back stunned. He needed time to grasp this in its entirety.

As Damayanti and Vidyadhar drank some more tea, Anveshak roused himself from his reverie and got out Gurudev's book that he had brought along and read:

> This finite, mortal, ever-changing world that we see around us is born out of Māyā alone. Due to non-apprehension of Reality, man recognizes the world of objects, emotions, and thoughts. Through the body, mind, and intellect, he contacts the world and creates more and more vāsanās. These vāsanās make one act more and more, and in the end, man becomes cocooned in them and gains permanently for himself the sense of a separate individuality, the jīvabhava. All these are created by this avidyā, the non-apprehension of Reality.

Looking up, Anveshak asked, "Māyā manifests itself as vāsanās created by avidyā, or as the glossary in the book tells me, lack of knowledge. Correct?"

"And the ignorance of all individuals grouped together is Māyā," agreed the professor.

"A deluded world," moaned Anveshak.

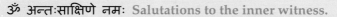

 ॐ अन्तःसाक्षिणे नमः Salutations to the inner witness.

In all panoramas of expressions, though It lends Existence to them, It remains as a mere Witness. For he is considered as the true witness of an incident who is not in the incident, but who happened to witness it, not from too far, with neither attachment nor aversion.

 Participate in all that happens in life, but do not become a partner!

"Do you understand what jīvabhava connotes here, Anveshak?" asked the yoginī.

"Ego. My ignorance creates a separate 'I,' which thinks of itself as the body, mind, and intellect."

"And away from the Self, or Brahman," reinforced the professor.

Anveshak wanted to continue the discussion, but noticing the professor glancing at his watch, he held back. Shortly after that, Professor Vidyadhar left to keep his next appointment.

Yoginī Damayanti observed Anveshak lost in his thoughts. Looking at the clock on the wall, she said, "Would you like to meet the Swamiji from Chinmaya Mission? I know he will be finishing his evening satsaṅga in another half hour. We could see if he is free after that."

Anveshak was more than willing, and when the two of them reached the āśrama, the discourse had just ended and people were streaming out of the satsaṅga hall. Anveshak was struck by the cheerful atmosphere of the place as people

ॐ विनयशीलाय नमः: Salutations to the one who is polite and humble.

When a senior Mahātmā visited the Sandeepany Ashram, Gurudev did not sit beside him. When asked, he said, "When he became a Saint, I was nobody. How can I sit equal to him?" Gurudev then sat at the Saint's feet and started massaging his legs.

Humility is a sign of wisdom. When knowledge unfolds, we realize how much we don't know.

walked out talking about what they had just heard. As they went into the hall, they spotted Swamiji standing and talking to a few people, addressing the doubts that had arisen in their minds after the talk.

On seeing Damayanti, Swamiji gestured to her to come closer. He greeted her with a warm smile and, "Hari Om!" as Damayanti prostrated at his feet. Moments later, she signaled to Anveshak to join them. From the way she introduced Anveshak, it was apparent that she had talked

about him previously to Swamiji. With humility he prostrated to Swamiji, who had a dignified bearing but was much younger than Anveshak had expected. Swamiji then showed him the large and beautiful Chinmaya center and informed him about the lectures that were held there, the hundreds of children who attended Bala Vihar classes, and the varied and multiple programs that were conducted to ensure that the philosophy of Vedānta was being transmitted to people of all ages and backgrounds.

ॐ वाग्मिने नमः **Salutations to the great orator.**

Till we subjectively gain a direct experience of the Self, all scriptural declarations are but empty noises and noisy emptiness produced for the sake of the students. Whatever scriptures we discuss, whatever discourses we hear or give, they are at best indirect knowledge, a mere blabber no matter how eloquent the talks may be. True eloquence is in Self-abidance, which in itself is a deep silence!

It is by exclusively choosing the Self alone that one can realize It, not by eloquence or mere study!

Damayanti, with a twinkle in her eyes, told Anveshak, "The right school, the right knowledge, all here!"

Smiling, Swamiji led them toward the temple adjoining the satsaṅga hall. All of them, after prostrating, sat by the altar, which had the deity of a tranquil Lord Śiva in the seat of meditation and a large picture of Gurudev, who, with a smile on his face, seemed to be leaning forward to hear them.

Anveshak, ever the seeker, was bubbling with questions but was hesitant about expressing himself in front of Swamiji. But with encouragement, he asked a bit timidly, "Swamiji, how does Māyā function?"

Swamiji said, "Through its properties of sattva, rajas, and tamas, which we call guṇās, or qualities of the mind. Each of them manifests itself differently."

"Since they hide the Self, are they all undesirable?"

"For the journey you are on, they are all to be transcended. But we will get to that. Do you know how these guṇās operate?" When Anveshak shook his head, Swamiji said, "These guṇās have unique characteristics and our thinking is shaped by them. Rajas creates thoughts of passion, tamas is dull and causes inertia, and sattva leads to pure and noble thoughts."

"Sorry, Swamiji, I don't understand. You said all the guṇas have to be transcended but sattva sounds desirable," said Anveshak.

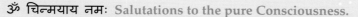

ॐ चिन्मयाय नमः Salutations to the pure Consciousness.

Consciousness is the one Reality at all times. When the thickness of vāsanās is increased, Its splendor in us seems to be dimmed. Therefore, it is meaningless to complain that my Consciousness was dull yesterday and that today it is bright.

The screen on which a movie is projected is unaffected by the quality of the picture shown on it. Shift your attention from the movie to the screen. You will discover stillness!

"Still, it is a property of Māyā, which veils the Self," pointed out Swamiji. "It has to be overcome, too."

"Is passion wrong?" asked Anveshak.

"Passion creates frenzied activity in the mind, which translates into action in the world. It creates the wrong interaction with objects, creates attachments and desire for more. It seeks sense gratification. We tend to act and react with restlessness and anxiety, and as you probably already know, this creates upheavals of joy and sorrow in us," said Swamiji.

Anveshak comprehended this, as he had been hearing about it from everyone who had been helping him on his journey.

Swamiji continued, "And what happens to the mind and body after feverish activity? We collapse in exhaustion. Damayanti tells me you were engaged in the stock market. Think of your days then. Passionate activity surely led to inertia."

"Dullness is definitely not a desirable state," observed Anveshak.

Swamiji said, "Tamas causes the intellect to be dull and indolent. When the intellect is in the strong grip of tamas, it does not allow the Self to shine through."

"The rajasic mind," continued Swamiji, "jumps to its own imagined construct and continues to emphasize sense gratification. Think of a flowing river. Can you see your reflection in it?"

"Not in flowing water, no. "

"If the river water were muddy, it would be even harder, correct?"

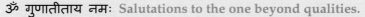 ॐ गुणातीताय नमः **Salutations to the one beyond qualities.**

Being unaffected by the three qualities of the mind, living a life of inward peace, independent of all environments, he enjoys the infinite joy of the Self.

 Mind is Māyā at play; be mindful about Māyā's mindless game!

Anveshak nodded.

"The water represents our thoughts, the continuous flow of water represents rajas, and the muddiness is tamas."

"And the reflection is the Self," said Anveshak.

"Exactly. The river of thoughts, which is our own mind, is the work of Māyā. Pūjya Gurudev says, 'Mind is Māyā at play.'"

Anveshak remembered Shantiji talking to him about conserving energy. With Swamiji's explanation it made more sense now. Anveshak also harked back to the time when at the height of his success, arrogant and tired, he had made several erroneous judgments in his business. It had led to more frustration as he had tried to prevent financial meltdown. Rajas and tamas, he thought. Agitator and veiler.

"What about sattva, Swamiji?" asked Anveshak.

"It is a reflector, a mirror. On the reflecting surface of sattva can be observed the clean or unclean mind and intellect," said Swamiji, "But remember, even clean water with no movement can show you only a reflection and not the original."

"Gurudev compared it to pure water. Let me tell you what he said about it," said Swamiji:

> When we say 'stinky water and muddy water,' we mean a specimen of pure water in which the stink and the mud are held in suspension. If the stink and the dirt are removed, the water again becomes pure. Similarly, sattva is always present, even in a tamasic man.

"So all three guṇās are in me?"

"In all of us, in different proportions."

"Are the proportions subject to change, or are we stuck with what we have?" asked Anveshak.

Damayanti spoke up softly, "Look at yourself, Anveshak. What do you think?"

Anveshak was amazed. Of course! He realized that his rajasic and tamasic qualities had indeed dwindled down."Does that mean the water is clearing up?" he asked lightly.

Swamiji smiled back at him. Damayanti said, "Thanks to your meditation and japa, Anveshak!"

Reflection: Swami Shantananda

One day, I approached Pūjya Gurudev with a doubt. Gurudev often spoke from the dais about surrender of the ego. This 'surrendering the ego part' I was not able to grasp. My problem was: How does one surrender? The very 'surrenderer' is our ego. How can ego surrender to the Lord? When I say I am surrendering, am I surrendering? This was my confusion. With this confusion in my mind, I asked, "Gurudev, how does one surrender the ego?" Immediately came the answer: "Surrender is not an ACT. It is an awareness born of understanding. The more you understand that there is a higher Power governing and directing your ego, ego slowly gets thinned down, and when the awareness becomes very clear and without doubt, then the real surrender takes place."

This was an eye-opener for me. That advice helped me to overcome the idea that one day I have to surrender to the Lord. It is a maturity born of awareness that the Lord is with me and He is the one running the show. The ego is a puppet in His hands. The ego gets automatically surrendered. But ego, being what it is, pops up now and then. But we are able to keep it under check once we are able to abide in this thought: the Lord is residing within us and He is in charge of our life.

Anveshak relaxed for a moment, but then another question popped up: "So, sattva is not sufficient to see the Self?"

"You need to transcend sattva, also," Swamiji reiterated what he had previously said.

"Professor Vidyadhar pointed out to me that the Self is changeless, which means It is not affected by thoughts. So It is free of guṇās, am I correct?"

"It is untainted, Anveshak."

"Should I be studying more to purify the mind, Swamiji?"

Swamiji repeated Gurudev's words: Mere erudition will never be sufficient. At best, it can puncture ignorance — but it cannot cut it down.

"Then what should I do?"

Swamiji again used the words of his Guru:

> In order to make the mind pure, one has to develop these two qualities [dispassion and discrimination]. By an intelligent self-denial of sense pleasures, dispassion will increase. By study, reflection, and contemplation upon the scriptures, discrimination will increase. When discriminative power is developed, it will help in increasing dispassion. When dispassion has increased, there will be a greater power of discrimination.

"I have understood about dispassion and detachment, and I have observed Dr. Sevadas at the office practicing this effortlessly. Now I

ॐ शास्त्रोद्धारकाय नमः Salutations to the one who revived the scriptures.

During moments of meditation, when we strive hard to experience the meaning of the Upaniṣad mantras, we are in the realm of contemplation. Through contemplation, our misunderstandings about ourselves, which are expressions of our ignorance, are removed. And when ignorance is banished, Knowledge shines forth.

Study of scriptures is an adventure. In this voyage, contemplation is the compass that guides one in the vast sea of Upaniṣad mantras.

understand dispassion is the condition that the ego should maintain. But, discrimination? I have always thought of it as something with negative connotations," said Anveshak.

"What do you mean?" asked the yoginī curiously.

"Discrimination against minorities, against the poor, people of color — you know what I mean," replied Anveshak.

"Well, consider it discrimination against the un-Real, and no one will fault you for being politically incorrect," laughed Swamiji.

Anveshak almost got it but wanted more clarity.

Swamiji pointed to Damayanti's ear lobes. "What is she wearing in her ears?"

"Diamond earrings," said Anveshak.

"How much would you pay for them?"

"I don't know much about diamonds, but I guess a few thousand dollars."

"Is that how much you paid?" Swamiji asked the yoginī.

"No!" she chortled. "It was more like fifteen dollars!"

"Looks like the original," said Anveshak with wide eyes.

"So is the world, Anveshak," said Swamiji, adding, "The ways of Māyā are inscrutable. You should see it clearly."

"I need to know the difference between the Real and un-Real!" cried Anveshak.

"That would be practicing discrimination!" said Swamiji joining the others in their laughter and enthusiasm.

"I cannot be fooled by what I see!" continued Anveshak.

"The mind is a trickster! Beware!" said Swamiji.

When they all sobered, Swamiji said, "When discrimination is developed and you see what is Real, your desires for the unnecessary, the unreal, will drop away and keep your heart and mind clear. And to be precise, Anveshak, Real is permanent and unreal is temporary. Think of what is permanent in you and in your life and what is not."

Anveshak dipped his head and tried to absorb all that he had heard.

"Study is important, Anveshak, but to go beyond dry theorizing — even more important, "Swamiji cautioned.

"Do you have pointers for me, Swamiji?"

Swamiji again quoted Gurudev:

> Therefore, learn not only to read, repeat, and understand, but to truly delve into and listen to the depths of yourself. Slip beyond the noisy frontier of your mind. Soar above the thundering agitations — the whirling, screaming thoughts. Just look quietly from within and watch all the blabbering. From the sequestered silence within yourself, be aware of the everything happening around and within, without involving yourself in any of it.

"Just be a witness," said Anveshak with understanding.

Happy to have had that spelled out, Damayanti turned to Anveshak and met his eyes. It was getting late, and they were very conscious of the time Swamiji had given them despite their unannounced arrival.

Once again they offered their praṇāms to Swamiji. And before they left, he gave Anveshak a book of Gurudev's writings as prasāda. "Mull over Gurudev's words," he advised.

Sādhanā

- Decrease attachments.
- Be a witness.
- Develop discrimination.
- Understand Ātman is untainted.

XXII

Sheaths: The Camouflage

Over the next several weeks, Anveshak read profusely and regularly attended discourses on the *Bhagavad-gītā* by Swamiji. He considered himself to be now working toward another Master's degree, this time on the Science of Life — after all, Vedānta had all the trademarks of the rationality of science! The college degree he had in economics, which he had until recently considered as defining his identity, was rapidly losing its glamor.

Anveshak also became a regular at the āśrama and was soon among the most cheerful and endearing of volunteers. He talked little, served more, and every chance he got, he sought solitude. It was not like he was forcing himself to not want fashionable clothes, or go to an acclaimed restaurant — he just wasn't interested anymore. His mind was preoccupied with serving, meditating, and study, and he was guided by Swamiji in applying Vedānta in his daily life.

One day, having finished his task at the āśrama bookstore, Anveshak went looking for Swamiji in the dining area, where he was having afternoon bhikṣā. Both Swamiji and the sevikā, who had prepared the meal, invited Anveshak to join in. As he ate the steamed vegetables and the light food that was free of garlic and butter, he was struck by a thought: Damayanti, as a practitioner of yoga, had once told him that food had qualities. She had said that being a vegetarian helped her in her meditation.

Anveshak looked at Swamiji, "Does being a vegetarian help with meditation? Is that why you are a vegetarian, Swamiji?" he asked, unable to wait for the meal to end to ask his question.

Not at all put out by the interruption, Swamiji said, "Food has guṇās, too. The *Bhagavad-gītā* says that consuming sāttvika foods goes toward creating sāttvika thoughts. If you struggle at any time with meditation, look back at what you might have eaten. It is likely your racing thoughts have been aided by it."

"It is one more tool, then, for self-control," said Anveshak.

"Yes, Gurudev pointed out that all religions enjoin followers to fast to enhance meditation power. 'Right food, right thought,' he said."

After the bhikṣā was over and he had helped the sevikā with cleanup, Anveshak followed Swamiji to the garden, hoping to get some time with him. As Swamiji watered the pots and worked among

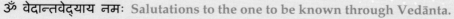

ॐ वेदान्तवेद्याय नमः Salutations to the one to be known through Vedānta.
The Upaniṣads constitute the literature of Vedānta, which shows the goal, declares the path, and gives the rational arguments for both. He who has learned it under the guidance of a Guru and follows the logic intelligently, alone can be proficient in Vedānta.

The Guru not only shows the path but establishes the logic of spirituality as well. Surrender at His feet!

the flower beds, he encouraged Anveshak to speak up if he had any questions.

"I have been reading that not only do we have multiple personalities and thoughts engendered by the three guṇās, but we also have three bodies and five sheaths in us that veil us from the Self!"

Swamiji was amused. "You don't like that?" he asked gently.

"I feel like Indiana Jones searching for the Holy Grail. It's one hurdle after another!"

"If I am not mistaken, your Indiana Jones found what he was looking for. But unlike him, Mr. Indiana Anveshak Jones, if you find what you are looking for, it will never slip out of your hands. You will never ever lose it! So it is worth it." Swamiji said, eyes sparkling.

Anveshak was a bit sheepish about his outburst, but with Swamiji patting him on the back, he ventured to ask, "Why is the Ātman veiled?"

"It is the power of Māyā again."

"It can be removed, then," said Anveshak.

Swamiji pointed to the water fountain in the garden. "Gurudev used moss as an example to explain the sheaths.

Reflection: Indra Advani

When Gurudev stayed in our home in 1975, he noticed some bottles of nail polish on my dresser and remarked, "You don't need these." Early next morning, while I drove him for his talks at Stanford University, he noticed my handbag and told me, "You do not need this." I stammered, "But Swamiji, I have to carry my driver's license, wallet...." He did not respond. Needless to say, nail polish dropped off easily. Then came the decision to downsize to a small two-bedroom apartment in a retirement community. To drop off this package of attachments, that is my sādhanā.

Imagine if the surface of the water over there were to be covered in moss. You wouldn't be able to see the water. Here is what Gurudev said:"

> When the moss is pushed aside by the hand, immediately the water manifests itself. But if one removes the hand and sits back even for a moment, thinking that all has been achieved, the moss, the Māyā, returns and covers the Self again by blanketing the reflective surface of the mind.

"The moss has to be removed as the purpose of the fountain was for the enjoyment of the water below," noted Anveshak. "I see the parallel with the Self and the sheaths."

"Do you understand what the five sheaths are, Anveshak?" asked Swamiji.

"Not fully, Swamiji. The sheaths that cover the Self, starting with the outermost, are the food sheath, air sheath, mind sheath, intellectual sheath, and the bliss sheath."

Swamiji nodded his head and said, "Let's see what each is about. This body, which makes up the outer sheath, is born of food — the seed of the father formed by the food he ate and nurtured in the womb of the mother by food. After birth, the body needs the nourishment of food to grow. And when the body dies, it goes back to the ground to become food for worms and plants."

"Just as food itself undergoes changes as it gets old, the body, too, changes with time," said Anveshak.

"With every thought and emotion, too, your body has changed. You are on a new journey right now. Observe yourself, and compare it to what it might have been when you were in business and then when you lost it."

Swamiji was right, reflected Anveshak. From his sartorial choices when he wore designer-label suits to the modest wear he preferred now; from his stylishly cut hair when he was a businessman to his grungy appearance when he was in despair; to the simple, clean look he had now — during each phase, his body had reflected his state of mind, including his demeanor and health, which had moved from aggressive to aggrieved and now to its present state of calm and unhurried emotions.

"What do you know about the air sheath?" asked Swamiji

"That, without it, the body would not be," said Anveshak. "Both are inert without the other."

"Yes," said Swamiji as he kneeled on the soil, weeding a bed of tulsī plants. "The air sheath is so vital for the body that Gurudev has described it as the 'Ātman' of the food sheath."

"It controls the food sheath," said Anveshak completing the thought.

"With age, it slows, and the five sense organs in the food sheath, through which stimuli of the world are taken in, slow down. So also do the five organs of action that work to satisfy those senses, including the limbs, the organs of speech, reproduction, and evacuation," said Swamiji.

"The body looks older and we are physically not capable of doing everything that we were capable of before," Anveshak said.

"As long as there is air in the body, all activities go on. When it leaves the body, everything halts," continued Swamiji.

"We die," said Anveshak

"Do we?" asked Swamiji, peering up at Anveshak.

"Oh! No, the body dies!" exclaimed Anveshak, tapping his forehead rapidly with his fingers for slipping back into his earlier understanding.

Swamiji, still bent over the tulsī plant, asked Anveshak, "Do you see that the air sheath is subtler than the food sheath?"

"Well, the body has a limited ability to go beyond a few feet in height or some inches in width,"continued Swamiji. "That's the extent to which its pervasiveness extends. But the air sheath, which powers the sense organs and the organs of action, excretion, digestion, circulation, and thinking can go beyond the confines of the body," explained Swamiji.

"But my eyes can see the sky, even though my body is here," said Anveshak.

"You're right," said Swamiji, "but even eyes have their limits. Listen on. The food and air sheaths together form the first of the three bodies you spoke of earlier. It is known in Vedānta as the gross body."

"I read what Gurudev said about it. He said, 'Fools consider themselves to be this packet of filth, consisting of skin, flesh, fat, and bones,'" Anveshak reported.

"So the shopping malls are full of people dazzled by the colors and smells that are being sold to satisfy this 'filth' — at least temporarily!" laughed Swamiji.

Anveshak sighed. He had been one of those. He remembered another description of the body by Gurudev: a cancerous growth on the Ātman!

ॐ तेजस्विने नमः Salutations to the brilliant one.

The Self is the Intelligence that illumines for us both the acts of commissions and omissions, meritorious or otherwise. It is again the Light Principle that illumines for us both our joys and sorrows. It is only a witnessing light of pure Intelligence lending its consciousness to the body, mind, and intellect. It does not participate in any of the transactions of life.

The brilliance in a brilliant person and the foolishness of the foolish — both are illumined by the One which is neither brilliant nor foolish!

Swamiji said, "Well, we have learned to use the body as Gurudev had explained — treat it as an instrument to work away the accumulated vāsanās."

Standing up, Swamiji washed his hands under the garden faucet and said, "Now let's go inward."As Anveshak instantly turned to do his bidding and go inside the āśrama, Swamiji repeated, "Inward, not in!"

Anveshak reddened. He had begun getting comfortable when talking to Swamiji, but his respect for Swamiji was deep, and a part of him did not want to reveal his ineptitude. He turned to see Swamiji giving him a genial smile.

But the learned Swami was not to be fooled."Did you feel a bit foolish just now?"

Anveshak merely nodded his head.

"In the light of what we have been conversing about, what caused that?"

With measured words Anveshak said, "My ego, attached to my mind and intellect."

"The spring board of 'I-ness and 'My-ness,'" said Swamiji. "Did that cause our peaceful talk to get disturbed?"

Anveshak had to agree.

"'I, the knower,' raised its head to point out that 'I' couldn't look foolish. 'My' image had to be protected," Swamiji detailed the moment of self-importance that had struck Anveshak.

As the young man continued to listen, Swamiji began walking around the garden checking the sprinklers."The ego is born and nurtured in the mind sheath and the intellectual sheath."

"If the mind is a continuous flow of thoughts, what is the intellect?" asked Anveshak.

"It is also made of thoughts," said Swamiji.

"Do those thoughts differ in quality?"

With Anveshak following him, Swamiji walked toward the rosebush growing in the shade of the āśrama wall. Lifting his hand, he lightly touched the plant, then pulled it back. "When my finger touched the plant, the skin felt the thorn and carried that sensation to the mind. The mind took it to the intellect, which, informed by past experiences, knows it's a thorn and tells the mind to withdraw the hand. The mind relays the matter to the hand."

"The intellect is the decision maker," said Anveshak.

"The mind flows through the sense organs. Without it, the eye cannot cognize the rose."

"The control centers of the sense organs are in the mind," said Anveshak.

"That the rose is beautiful, and it is red, are things that the eye sees."

"The mind sheath pervades the gross body. It is subtler," said Anveshak.

"It is also subtler than air because by a thought you can pause breathing as well."

"Yes."

"Right now, I am debating whether I should pick the rose and take it in for the evening pūjā or let it flourish here."

"So the mind vacillates, correct? And then the intellect makes a

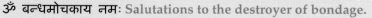

ॐ बन्धमोचकाय नमः Salutations to the destroyer of bondage.

He who is reveling, traveling in his own experience, is one who, unasked, helps others to cross the shores of delusion and sorrow. Therefore, to surrender to such a one, requesting him to save us from our misunderstandings, is to assure for ourselves a true liberation — almost like boarding a luxury liner to Truth!

Just as one floating log is sufficient to cross a river, surrender to one Guru for liberation!

decision based on experiences in the past." Anveshak was beginning to understand the differences between mind and intellect.

"The intellect is 'I — the knower.' It goes beyond just past experiences. It has no frontiers," said Swamiji.

Anveshak decided not to continue with their unique method of communication, where Swamiji would make a statement and he would zero in on the meaning.

Swamiji said, "Scientific ideas, great authorship, new ideologies are born in the intellect. It can dream, it can construct new worlds."

"The mind cannot?" asked Anveshak.

"The mind is limited by things known, it does not function in the unknown. It can recall a vacation you have had in Hawaii, but it cannot imagine the people of Aruba or Fiji if you have not visited there."

"The intellect is capable of so much and yet it doesn't see the true Self?" asked Anveshak.

Swamiji recalled Gurudev's words:

> The intelligence is there only because of the Consciousness playing through the intellect in us. The matter-equipment, the intellect, becomes brilliant because of the Light of Consciousness. The intellect by itself has no intelligence. It is like a mirror in darkness.

Swamiji paused and then continued:

> The intellect, due to the Light of Consciousness playing in it, develops the capacity to illumine things projected by the mind, and as a final result of all these, it comes to identify with the body, the senseorgans, and so on. It becomes the restless ego, the 'I-ness,' and identifying with the objects perceived by the sense organs, it provides the 'My-ness.'

"So when the Self projects itself through the intellect, it becomes the ego?" asked Anveshak

"Consciousness does not become ego. Remember It is unconditioned — always. When it is reflected through the intellect, the intellect assumes that it is itself the source of light and identifies with the rest of the apparatus. This identification and attachment make up the ego," clarified Swamiji.

When Anveshak looked like he might have understood, Swamiji moved on to explain that the mental and intellectual sheaths together form the subtle body. "The mind and intellect, along with sensory faculties that perceive the world, constitute the subtle body," he said.

Anveshak asked, "Please explain how to develop dispassion to overcome the subtle body."

"Gurudev suggested this:"

Dispassion for a thing will develop only when one finds that the object no more gives one any joy. If the idea that the joy-content is not in the object outside is firmly established in one's understanding, then one is immediately released from all of one's personality bondages. This dispassion is brought about by the intellect alone."

Anveshak said not a word after this, lost in all that he had learned, quietly helping Swamiji finish the rest of his work in the garden. Swamiji then led him to the fountain and seated himself on its stone edge. "There is one more sheath and one more body you should know about," he said.

"The bliss sheath and the causal body," murmured Anveshak.

"They are one and the same," said Swamiji. "It is the closest to the Ātman and because of that the most subtle. There are mere ripples of thoughts there."

Anveshak perked up. "Mere ripples of thoughts! That's why it is known as the bliss sheath." Then, moderating his excitement, he said, "But it is still Māyā's handiwork. There must be a catch here."

"It is a state of utter and total ignorance," said Swamiji, waiting to see Anveshak's reaction.

"I have heard the saying, ignorance is bliss! But ignorance is what we are trying to fight," said Anveshak.

"It is a collection of all your vāsanās which have not been affected by the agitation of thoughts," said Swamiji.

"Does the Self identify with it?" asked Anveshak after giving it some thought.

"It manifests as the deep sleeper. Gurudev explains as follows:"

> Ordinarily we are used to the endless stress and strain in our daily life. That moment in our life when our agitations are comparatively less, is a relatively happy moment. So the happiest moment is that in which there are but negligible agitations in our bosom. These small thoughts are said to be bliss thoughts.

"So there is happiness to be found there?" asked Anveshak.

ॐ ब्रह्मपराय नमः: Salutations to the one for whom Brahman alone is supreme.

The supreme goal is the realization of our identity with the All-soul, the Brahman. With this true identification, the false identifications with the mind-intellect equipment, the ego sense in total, ends. We cannot have the knowledge of the rope and the serpent at one and the same time: so, too, Knowledge of the Self and the ego.

Realizing the Oneness of all beings cannot be pursued by holding on to the ego. Don't hesitate to throw the light on the rope to let go of the notion of a snake!

"What is experienced is not happiness, but absence of sorrow. It is a sheer state of non-apprehension of the Self."

"Am I experiencing this when I wake up on some mornings feeling rested and energized because I have slept so well?" asked Anveshak.

"That is precisely it. Dreamless sleep," said Swamiji.

"Do the gross and subtle bodies identify with the Self, too?' asked Anveshak.

"The Self, Gurudev said, 'seemingly expresses itself through the three bodies to create the human personality — the waker-dreamer-sleeper.' As the waker with the gross body and as the dreamer with the subtle body," Swamiji said.

"What are dreams, Swamiji?" asked Anveshak.

"'Dreams come from incomplete actions and thoughts during the day. They are suppressions and reparations that have gone into the mind undigested.' That was Gurudev's explanation," said Swamiji.

"That doesn't sound good at all," said Anveshak.

"The brain only rests during deep sleep, so if it spends the night roaming about from one dream to another, it never really recoups its full intellectual capacity. A mind working constantly day and night becomes dull, or mad."

"Does Gurudev show us how to stop uninterrupted dreaming?" asked Anveshak.

"It is not your choice. However, you can try reducing it. Gurudev had many tips for us. Listen to some of them:"

There is no need to dream if you consciously and completely face each situation during the day. Until you have the ability to accomplish this continuous mental cleaning during the day, you can complete two rounds of japa beads with your mantra before you go to sleep at night. This practice will bring up all the undigested thoughts of the day.

Anveshak looked thoughtful again. At first he did japa as suggested by Shantiji to focus on God, then the yoginī had asked him to do the same to reduce his thoughts, and now japa was to get rid of dreams?

Swamiji waited. Nothing. Realizing that Anveshak may have trouble formulating his next question, he stated boldly, "The waking world is a dream, too."

That got him a quick gasp from Anveshak. What?! Anveshak was not sure he had heard right. "Am I not sitting here? Are you talking to me in my dreams, Swamiji? I feel the air on my body, I smell the flowers...."

Swamiji laughed. Anveshak stopped his rant.

"Where does the dream happen?"

"In the mind," said Anveshak.

"Who creates the dream world?"

"The mind," said Anveshak.

"Who is having the dream experience?"

"I am"

"Which 'I'?"

Anveshak thought. It couldn't be the Real 'I' as it is unaffected. It had to be the conditioned 'I.' "The mind," he said.

"Are you saying this is true of the waking state, too?" asked a flabbergasted Anveshak, leaping to his feet.

"All a hallucination of the mind," said Swamiji with great equanimity.

If it had been the yoginī, doctor, or the professor, Anveshak knew he would have stomped off in irritation or argued heatedly. With Swamiji, whom he held in the highest esteem, he did not know what to do.

"What, no smart repartee?" asked Swamiji, laughing again. When Anveshak stood looking bemused, Swamiji quoted Gurudev:

> In deep sleep, when the mind ceases to function, where are the objects of the world, their charms, or their plurality? What happens then to the pain of bereavement or the joy of success? When the mind functions, the outer world flares up with its burden of imperfections, limitations, decay, and death. When the mind is at rest, the world dissolves into nothingness.

Anveshak was still reeling. Nothing was real. Everything he had considered real was a construct of the mind.

> So then, this world of variable experiences of man, this woeful life of plurality and its sorrows, is projected by man's mind alone. Consequently, this world is of the mind alone; de facto, it is not there.

Anveshak felt Māyā was a sadist. Why am I here? If this whole thing — the body, mind, intellect, vāsanās, ignorance — are unreal, then who am I? Am I real or an illusion? Who knows this illusion? How can illusion cover the Real?

All these imagined experiences, tears, pain. For what purpose?

Sādhanā

- Remember: the body is merely an instrument to destroy vāsanās.
- Don't try to find lasting joy in objects.
- Remind yourself the world is a construct of the mind.
- Understand Brahman is untainted.

XXIII

Brahman: The Indescribable

During the early days of Anveshak's inner quest, the restlessness that had set him on this journey of finding the Self had caused him agony. "I can no more carry on with daily experiences when I know them to be unreal," Anveshak thought to himself. "If all that happened in the past and all that will be happening in my life are illusion, then what am I busy with? For what purpose is eating and drinking if my body itself is unreal? How can I interact with others if they all are my mind's construct?" Anveshak was unable find any answer.

When he had missed his fiancée, he had been able to distract his mind with other things. But few things other than the quest he was on, drew his attention any more.

Then, one day while at the āśrama, he dropped the cleaning cloth in his hand and rushed out into the āśrama garden as if seeking release from the pain of intense emptiness within. He gulped back tears. Hands on hips, he threw his head back, staring up into the evening sky. What was going on? Why couldn't he find the peace he was seeking? He shook a finger at the sky as if admonishing it. Swamiji, who was passing by in the corridor that overlooked the garden, stopped on seeing Anveshak. Moments later, Anveshak noticed him. The compassion on Swamiji's face helped soothe the pain. Reverently, he touched Swamiji's feet. Without a word exchanged, the two headed to the meditation room. In the quiet and in the presence of the picture of Gurudev, Anveshak felt his pain subside some more.

Noticing his return to calm, Swamiji said quietly, "Gurudev once said that the sun shines without differentiation on all — you, me, the flowers, worms, the garbage dump — it is for us to open our windows and doors and let the sun in to enjoy its blessings. You are doing that, Anveshak."

Engrossed in his own thoughts, Anveshak sat down, which was not something that he would do normally, as he was too respectful to sit unless bidden by Swamiji. But Swamiji sat down, too. After a while, Swamiji asked, "If your clothes were on fire right now, what would you do, Anveshak?"

"Try to put it out quickly."

"How?"

"I would get water as quickly as possible," said Anveshak.

"Because you don't want to burn."

"That would be my only intention," said Anveshak.

"To get to the water would be your only thought."

"Or I would burn." Anveshak paused. "Or I would be in pain. I am in pain. I don't want to deal with the world anymore. Everything is false, unreal! To get to the Self is my only thought."

"You are what we call a mumukṣu — someone who has an urgent desire to get to the Self, with the same pressing urgency that someone has to put out a fire."

ॐ अजाय नमः Salutations to the unborn one.

He, the Supreme, on account of His unquestioned freedom, by His own perfect free will, takes upon Himself the conditioning matter, and manifests Himself in a particular embodiment in the world, for serving the deluded generation of that time. His 'ignorance' is but a pose assumed, not a fact lived.

You are not your body; you wear this body as apparel.

"There will be pain," said Anveshak. "How do I deal with a world that is unreal?"

Swamiji smiled. "It is unreal, Anveshak, but not non-existing."

What? Anveshak was visibly confused. Unreal cannot exist!

"What is the color of the sky?" Swamiji asked.

"Blue," replied Anveshak and immediately added, "but not always...at night it becomes dark!"

"You see a blue sky knowing well that the sky is not blue. Do you have any problem with that?"

"No." Anveshak could comprehend what Swamiji was trying to convey. "You mean I can continue to deal with the world though it is unreal?"

"You continue to experience the world but need not give reality to what you experience. When you think it is real, it becomes a part of the impressions that you have already gathered."

"Vāsanās," said Anveshak. "When do all impressions — which create desires to experience the world — die?"

"Till that desire to be liberated from the subtle body is not yet fulfilled. This subtle body is what is known as the soul, which comes back again and again to experience the world."

"Rebirth!" Anveshak's face suddenly lit up. When all desires end, then there is discovery of immortality — no birth!

ॐ अव्ययाय नमः **Salutations to the imperishable one.**

Keeping His Māyā perfectly under His own control, all the time, He is fully conscious of His own divine status and unchallenged prerogative. He does not come into being as others do, compelled by His past Karma, to live here in the world under the thralldom of Nature. He is not bound by His mental temperaments; but He is ever free from the mischiefs of His own Māyā.

Often, consciously decide your thoughts; let not your thoughts define you!

"But going back to what you said, 'desire to be liberated from the subtle body' — aren't desires an impediment?" asked Anveshak, who equated the word 'desire' as something to be erased from his spiritual dictionary.

Looking at the picture of Gurudev on the wall, Swamiji recounted Gurudev's words:

> True, it is an ego-centered desire, as are all desires. However, this is a higher desire, so you may keep it. When all desires have been removed, it will die of itself because it cannot exist when all desires have disappeared.

"This desire to be the Self will die when all other desires die?" asked Anveshak. "So this desire is a tool, too."

Swamiji said, "The desire to realize the Self is the desire to be desireless!" He smiled, patted Anveshak gently, and exited the meditation room, leaving him with enough to ponder upon. Anveshak struggled to understand.

Anveshak went home that night, heavy of heart. He searched the books that had been given to him by Swamiji and found this by Gurudev:

> In our scriptures, there is not just one creation story. Each sage told his bluff story in order to clear the confusion of a particular student. He pointed only to the apparent creation — the creation in the student's mind. These explanations were to clear a particular question and for that purpose alone. That is why there are so many different theories.

Anveshak was struck by several things. Personalized education! There was no linear learning in Vedānta: explanations were provided based on the individual's questions. What the questions were depended on the way the maze of the mind worked. It was why he kept reading about the importance of the Guru. No matter how much he read himself, he had felt the need to seek someone with a deeper understanding to remove ambiguity.

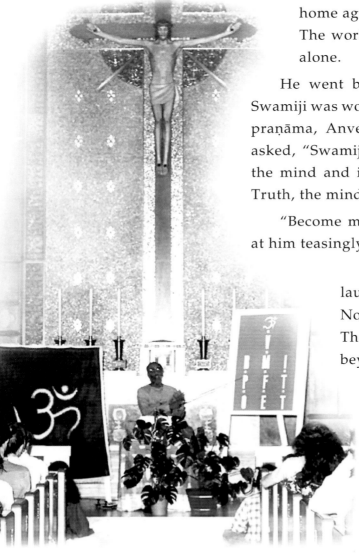

Gurudev's words also brought home again what Swamiji had told him. The world was a construct of the mind alone.

He went back to Swamiji the next day. Swamiji was working at his desk. After offering praṇāma, Anveshak took a deep breath and asked, "Swamiji, if the world is a creation of the mind and is in the way of getting to the Truth, the mind has to be overcome, yes?"

"Become mindless!" said Swamiji looking at him teasingly.

Anveshak blinked. Then he laughed. "I have to lose my mind! No one has told me that before." Then he asked, "How does one get beyond the mind?"

Swamiji gestured to Anveshak to seat himself and told him a story of Gurudev's personal experience. "When Gurudev was trying to decide whether he should become a monk or not, he went to Badrinath to do some soul-searching. One day, as he stood

Gurudev giving a discourse on BMI
at a church in the U.S.

praying in front of Lord Nārāyaṇa, an American visitor interrupted him and asked him what the idol was made of. Gurudev was stunned. He had no idea. For him it was Lord Nārāyaṇa, nothing else mattered. Much later, after he had become a Swami, he was in Europe where he visited a church. Looking at the large cross on the wall, he asked a church member what kind of wood had been used to make the cross!"

"Look deeply to find the essence," deduced Anveshak.

"Become an observer of the outside world and yourself," advised Swamiji.

"What am I to observe in myself?" asked Anveshak.

"When someone talks to you, you reply. But also note your intellect's response and the mind's emotions."

"Stand back and become a witness. What is the goal with this kind of observation?" asked Anveshak.

"To turn the gross intellect into the subtle intellect."

"I don't understand, Swamiji," said Anveshak.

An avid gardener, Swamiji used an example close to his heart to illustrate his point, "When we see an earthworm, we think of it contemptuously as just a worm, but if we pay more attention, we know it is a friend of all farmers because it oxygenates the soil. A finer intellect will see it as a living thing, and an even subtler intellect will perceive it for it is — a divine thing with the same Spark of Existence in it as in you and me."

ॐ अविनाशिने नमः Salutations to the indestructible one.

He is That which envelops everything that exists and which is the very stuff and substance of all the worlds of perceptions which we experience. None — not even God — can destroy Him, the Self of all!

Silently watch the perishing nature of matter while abiding as changeless Awareness!

Anveshak nodded in understanding. Swamiji explained further with Gurudev's words:

> The attempt of the spiritual seeker is to plunge to a new depth in himself and from there to look out upon the world and continue to expand those depths. Not to remain there, but to grow, rise, and to see with new eyes. This deeper level of seeing is the purpose of all sādhanā.

As Anveshak ruminated, Swamiji quietly returned to his writing.

"How can I practice this 'deeper level of seeing,' Swamiji?"

Swamiji looked up and pointed toward the large oil canvas of Lord Dakshinamurthy hanging on the wall. "Why don't you sit in front of the painting and just look at it."

Anveshak sat down on the carpeted floor. The painting caught his eye, as its subject was beautifully illumined by the light that poured in through the large windows in Swamiji's room. He studied the painting and noted the figures in it. Then he noticed the expressions on the faces of the figures, then the varied hues of the leaves of the tree under which the Lord sat. And whatever he observed, his mind cataloged — it was a nonstop stream of thoughts, akin to the play-by-play commentary at a basketball game.

After a while, Swamiji, noticing Anveshak's eyes roaming more slowly over the painting, softly said, "Start to shift your attention to the canvas itself. Just your attention, not your eyes!"

Reflection: Swami Dheerananda

I received a letter from Śrī Gurudev at Sandeepany Sadhanalaya that detailed the daily routine that I must follow while I was to be at Tapovan kuṭīra. "Do Gāyatrī Japa 1,000 times in the morning. Eat one meal a day. Study in the afternoon. Contemplate once the sun sets in the evening." Gurudev's words in that letter were tattooed in my mind.

How? Every inch of the canvas was covered in paint. How was he to see it? Anveshak did not find it easy. His mind pulled him back again and again to the visuals on the canvas. But he did as Swamiji had instructed and patiently sat, gazing at the painting. In time, everything seemed to dissolve, and he found that he could see just the canvas, hidden behind the colors.

He heard Swamiji saying softly, "Now, shift your attention to the eyes which are seeing the canvas. Don't close your eyes." Anveshak did not understand. What was he to see? How could the eyes see the eyes? Then, with sudden clarity, he understood that it was not about the eyes! Swamiji had spoken of shifting 'attention.' It was the mind! He had to get his mind to shut out all other thoughts. He resolved to ignore his questioning mind. Soon, he had an all-consuming thought and he said aloud, "I am seeing."

Moments later, Swamiji, in a soft voice, directed him to let go of that thought, too, and focus on, 'I am.'

Anveshak remained silent. Swamiji waited.

Anveshak struggled to not have the compelling thought of "I am seeing." But it slowly subsided, and he felt a strange but deep calmness dawning in him.

"Anveshak?" the low tones of Swamiji's voice called out to him. 'I am.' Anveshak struggled to speak. 'I am.' He did not want to leave the experience of deep silence. Then it hit him, 'I am' had not been a thought! But how to retain this? Do I need a picture in front of me to focus and defocus? Is this thoughtless stillness anywhere close to the experience of the Self?

A long time later, the only sound in the room was the tapping of the keyboard on Swamiji's desk. The sound was broken by a diffident Anveshak asking, "What will there be when thoughts are transcended?"

"Pure Existence, which is Self-aware of its own blissful nature."

"Does OM in Gurudev's BMI chart represent this?"

"Yes, it does. OM is the sound symbol of the Self. Gurudev suggested that during meditation one should turn the mind exclusively to the Self, and one can effectively use this sound symbol for focusing on the Self."

'How?"

Swamiji silently got up and sat in a lotus pose next to him on the floor. After adjusting himself, he closed his eyes and softly chanted OM with his deep voice. Anveshak closed his eyes and listened to the chanting.

"Listen to the silence between two OM utterances," said Swamiji after chanting OM a few times.

Anveshak, who already had had the glimpse of deep silence, could feel the stillness within himself. He chanted along with Swamiji. The repeated chanting slowly ended in long gaps of silence. Anveshak could easily dive into the silence. No thoughts.

ॐ ओंकारविदे नमः **Salutations to the knower of Om.**

Om does not define the highest Reality. For, to define It is to defile It. In the technique of self-perfection, the symbol Om is at once a formula indicating the goal and a symbol for the purpose of worship of Brahman and for meditation. To a meditator, if Om represents the total Mind, he gains Brahma-loka, and if it represents supreme Reality, through the power of concentration, eventually realizes the Self as "This I am."

A symbol represents the ideal that inspires the meditator. By consistent practice alone, the symbol will merge into [reveal] the ideal.

Moments later when he opened his eyes, he saw Swamiji smiling at him. "Pure existence," Anveshak slowly repeated what he heard before.

"I still have a doubt: if Ātman is of the nature of Brahman, Ātman, too, has to be sat, cit and ānanda, right?" asked Anveshak.

"In a limited manner, in the gross body, the Self expresses itself as existence, or sat; in the subtle body, as cit, or intelligence; and in the causal body, as ānanda, or bliss. So what is expressed as sat-cit-ānanda is the Ātman. Truth has neither sat, cit, or ānanda. Remember these are three aspects of the same, they are not characteristics," pointed out Swamiji.

"All in one?"

"Pure Existence is self-aware, which means it is conscious of its own existence without any aid. Also, being independent of all matter, it is bliss — ānanda!"

Swamiji waited. With a faraway look in his eyes, Anveshak thought aloud, "The world as I know it now, with the body, mind, and intellect, will not be there. If it is not there, then its experiences are not there either. Only the changeless Ātman remains. And the Ātman is Brahman." Anveshak went back to thinking.

Swamiji continued to wait. It was a while until Anveshak's hushed voice filled the silent room, "Because the Ātman is separated from Brahman by Māyā...." Overcome, he stopped speaking. Then he

ॐ कैवल्य-स्वरूपाय नमः Salutations to the one whose nature is Reality.

That which existed even before the Creator was born to create the pluralistic world, and that which is unconditioned by time and place, must necessarily be the Absolute One which is all-pervading and formless. It has to be all-pervading because there existed nothing other than Itself!

Loneliness is the feeling of being left alone; whereas, for the wise, alone-ness is a consciously cherished solitude!

continued, his face flushed with excitement, "Just like a river loses its identity when it joins the ocean. The river does not remain. There is nothing left of the river and there is nothing left of the Ātman! Yes? Isn't it?"

Swamiji's eyes crinkled in enjoyment.

"Let's say the mind has been overcome, what happens where the mind was?" asked Anveshak.

Swamiji reached out for the table calendar on the desk and pushed it toward Anveshak. "That is a picture of the Grand Canyon. Do you think it is still where it was when the picture was taken?"

"Swamiji!" Anveshak protested, thinking he was being teased. "Of course!"

"The Grand Canyon remains where it is, and yet the image you hold in your hands is also the Grand Canyon," said Swamiji, once again gently pushing Anveshak to think and infer.

"Where the mind was, Brahman was. And is," said Anveshak, "There is only a shift in realization."

"The Truth is all-pervading and you and I are in it."

"Can you illustrate this for me, Swamiji?" asked Anveshak, after trying to grasp the enormity of it.

Swamiji bent his head and began writing on a piece of paper, then said, "Gurudev had the best analogy, I reproduce it here. Imagine a piece of woven cloth with a garden pattern on it," he turned the paper so Anveshak could see what he had written:

Cotton: Brahman

Thread: God

Garden pattern: world

Individual flower: individual

Anveshak studied it as Swamiji began to speak. "If we look at a single flower in the garden pattern or just a leaf, it is like being aware of the individual — you and I. If we stand back and look at the entire pattern, the garden emerges; that is the world. You see the larger picture." Anveshak comprehended so far.

"The whole pattern is woven on the piece of cloth. The cloth and the embroidered pattern on it are created by threads. Remove the thread and the whole thing will unravel; there will be no cloth and no world. The thread is God," said Swamiji. He continued, "The thread is not self-born. Where did it come from?"

"Cotton." Then Anveshak said, "In the thread is the cotton, and from cotton comes the thread. All is born of Brahman."

"Is the nose on your face separate from your body?"

"I cannot be born of Brahman as that would assume I am separate from Brahman." Anveshak reframed his sentence, "All is Brahman."

Anveshak wondered: How powerful and enormous was this Brahman that it could encompass so much?

Swamiji laughed and said, "Defining it in human terms, are we?"

"The mind is limited by its experience," Anveshak connected the subject under discussion to what he had learned earlier.

"Well then, it is like nothing you know. Brahman's ID card will have no gender, size, color, shape, form. So it's just IT."

ॐ जीवब्रह्मैक्यविदे नमः Salutations to the Knower of the oneness of the individual and the Supreme.

To realize one's own Self is to realize, at once, Its oneness with the All-Self. To realize the nature of a wave is to realize not only the nature of all the waves, but the very nature of the ocean. Life being one and unbroken, to experience the Life-center within us is to experience at once the Life-center everywhere.

Pursuit of Self-realization is not a selfish endeavor; it eventually includes all beings, leaving none behind.

"You are only telling me what it is not," pointed out Anveshak.

"The mind and intellect cannot grasp It. Even in the Vedas, Truth is not described. It is only indicated. Gurudev said:"

> Necessarily therefore, the language of the marketplace, the words of the drawing room, the phrases of the slums, the slang of the drinking booth can never hope to express the Perfect and the Immortal. Language cannot define, cannot even vaguely report upon the transcendental experience which one comes to live in the stillness of one's own mind. To define Truth, therefore, is to defile Truth.

Anveshak suddenly recalled, "Professor Vidyadhar said the Absolute was Transcendental, Supreme…."

Swamiji broke in, "Real, One-without-a-second, Pure, Knowledge, Devoid-of-beginning-and-end, Immeasurable, Irreducible, Self-effulgent, Self-existent."

"Swamiji!' Anveshak's head spun.

"Omniscient, Omnipresent, Omnipotent."

"Indescribable!" said Anveshak. "And to be experienced!"

Sādhanā

- Be an observer of your thoughts.
- Remind yourself that all is Brahman.
- Chant 'Om' and dwell in silence.

XXIV

Samādhi: Cessation of 'I'

The destination could not be described.

On discovery, the destination would reveal itself as 'Pure Existence.'

For Anveshak, the journey was already proving to be a challenging one. And yet here he was, trying to get there. Someone unfamiliar with all this would have called him crazy.

Arms on hips, Anveshak stood staring at the setting sun from the balcony of his apartment. Was this thing even worth it, given the improbabilities? How and when had the quest for a little bit of peace turned into full-blown hunger for something more enduring and lasting? The sky turned inky, and yet Anveshak stood where he was, tossing and turning things in his mind.

His thoughts went to what he had read earlier to see if he could find an answer to something he was curious about: If Truth could not be described, how was the seeker to know that he had realized the Absolute? He pondered this analogy by Gurudev:

> It is as though all the waves of the ocean have suddenly stopped at the magic wave of a wand, as though they have been stunned into freezing.

He recalled his experience of shifting attention from the painting to the canvas to the eyes and getting to a state of thoughtlessness. It must mean that it was a state where there was no activity, physical, mental, or intellectual, Anveshak figured. Is it possible to remain in that state? Though Swamiji had never ever shown an iota of disinterest or annoyance at Anveshak's questions, he felt guilty taking Swamiji away from his āśrama work. He wondered if he should go to the professor with his doubts, but Vidyadhar had plainly, but not unkindly, said that Anveshak's questions were getting significant, and that he would be best served by the learned Swami.

The next day, the trepidation he felt was banished immediately when Swamiji welcomed him with a warm, "Hari Om! Here is our young seeker!"

As Anveshak stood with hands folded in a namaskāra, Swamiji asked, "What questions do you bring today?"

On seeing that there were indeed things that Anveshak wanted to ask, Swamiji led the way to the altar, where the pūjā had just finished and the fragrance of incense wafted in the air.

"If the realized person is engaging in no activity, does that mean such a person goes into seclusion?" Anveshak asked urgently.

"It does not mean the person necessarily runs off to sit in a cave. The realized one could do that or walk and work among us. Gurudev came down from the Himalayas to spread the greatest philosophical truths to whoever would listen. He came for our benefit. What happens is that the realized person sees the world differently."

ॐ अद्वितीयाय नमः **Salutations to the One-without-a-second.**

The ultimate Reality, being One-without-a-second, cannot of its very nature have anything to do with one or the other of any conceivable pairs of opposites. Vice has got an existence only with reference to virtue; light can be recognized only with reference to darkness; life would be meaningless without death.

From the standpoint of relativity, the ultimate Reality is a hypothesis. Upon realization, relativity reveals itself to be only mental activity!

"Does the world exist for him? If there is no world, there can be no God either, isn't that true?" Anveshak reasoned.

"Gurudev started out as an atheist. Do you think he reverted to becoming one again after his Vedānta studies?" Swamiji laughed. "Conversely, he became a great devotee of God! He admired the ultimate Reality that makes this illusory world appear so real, enchanting, beautiful, and unfathomable."

"Is that what makes a saint enjoy everything, accept everyone, and love unconditionally?"

"Yes. However, saints also know how to withdraw into utter silence when not interacting in the world."

"How?"

"They know that the One who creates the world is the very One who witnesses it as well. When the saints withdraw within, they abide in that One from which everything came and merge into It.

"And how do they interact with the world after that? With dispassion and detachment?" asked Anveshak.

"And with overflowing love, as having transcended the mind, they don't see plurality. Gurudev gave the example of us accidently poking our eye with our finger. The eye is hurt, but will we cut off of our finger to punish it?"

"We won't because it is part of us, and it would cause us pain to hurt ourselves." Anveshak surmized, then stated with full understanding, "The realized person sees no difference between himself and the world."

"Listen to what Gurudev said:"

When one has realized that the Reality within him is the pith and substance that constitute all others in the universe, love and kindness are natural and continuous in his bosom for all in the world.

"Will I be able to recognize such a person?" asked Anveshak.

"Again, I recount Gurudev's words:"

It is one of the surest symptoms of knowledge and saintliness if we can observe an individual who is, under all provocative circumstances, infinitely at peace with himself and with the world.

"Swamiji, how does one overcome thoughts for good?" Anveshak's question was laced with some desperation. He had experienced a wondrous state of thoughtlessness with an experiment guided by Swamiji, but he wanted to experience that forever, doing away with all battles with the mind.

The only way to transcend the mind is to contemplate. Through devotion, turn emotional thoughts to Him. Through rational thinking, contemplate on Him.

"That was Gurudev's short answer. You are already focused and thinking deeply. It is evident that's why you seek to find answers," said Swamiji encouragingly.

"Contemplate," said Anveshak, recalling his conversations with Professor Vidyadhar.

Swamiji said, "Gurudev's advice was to sit down and consciously withdraw the mind as though in sleep and experience that stage where there is no object, emotion, or thought."

"The key word is consciously, isn't it? Because in deep sleep the world disappears, but we are no closer to the Supreme," said Anveshak.

"Objectless Awareness is what Gurudev called it."

"You mean Thoughtless Awareness?"

"Let me clarify this for you. In the early stages of practice, you need to quieten the mind by reducing the number of thoughts through specific means. Then comes the practice of letting go of the mind."

"I did experience it by shifting my attention from the painting."

"Yes, but that was only for a short time, as you got a glimpse of the state of no-mind. Gurudev's advice to us is to practice constant vigilance in daily life to discard the mind as false."

Of course it was easier understood than practiced. Swamiji had told Anveshak what Gurudev had prescribed as a first step:

> In the contrast between what we actually are and what we believe ourselves to be is the first great hurdle we need to overcome as aspirants. Introspection, or self-analysis, is the only means to relieve this initial block. Self-evaluation is the only method to knowing ourselves.

And, for Anveshak, it was like wrestling a ferocious tiger. Honest self-examination was a brutal process. On some days, he was able to bring the mind to total stillness, and most other days he simply felt maimed. It was horrible and disagreeable as he did not like what he saw of himself. Was there going to be an end to this?

ॐ ब्रह्मनिष्ठाय नमः Salutations to the one established in Brahman.

Spirituality is not something that we can start discussing and arguing about among ourselves to while away an idle hour. It is to be understood in an atmosphere of peace and tranquility; for the understanding is an attempt at comprehending the deep experiences of the Master, expressed not so much through his words as perhaps through the ring of sincerity that the words carry when they come from his heart, throbbing with his own niṣṭhā (abidance).

Words cannot fully express the spiritual experience. By abiding in the Self, you go closer to the Master's vision of Reality.

He called Shantiji. Her kind words were always a balm for him. And once again, she stepped up to his need. Gently, she told him to keep on the path. "Gurudev has said that all this unpleasantness is only for a short time, Anveshak. He says it gets 'entertaining' and 'profitable!' It will get easier."

"I don't know what Gurudev means by a short time, but I feel like I have been doing this forever and am still not able to maintain the state of no-mind," complained Anveshak.

Shantiji, with a smile in her voice, told him what Gurudev had said in a discourse on the *Gītā* about this kind of impatience:

> 'Swamiji there is no progress at all even after three years,' you say. Okay, do you know how many pounds of food you have eaten in those three years? What happened to the rest of it? Miracle of miracles! So much food went in, nothing remained there. Similarly, only a small percentage of the effort you put in will stay.

Anveshak sighed. "Gurudev is funny, and he is right. Okay, Shantiji. Thank you as always," he said as he hung up the phone.

One evening after satsaṅga, he asked Swamiji to explain what self-evaluation would do for him.

"If done with complete honesty, it will overcome the mind. However, the practice of samādhi is very important," Swamiji told him.

He was no saint! Only monks practiced this 'samādhi' thing, didn't they? Did he have to learn to die?

Swamiji laughed, "In a way, yes. The 'I' should die."

"Ah!" was Anveshak's smart response.

Swamiji continued, "Samādhi means that practice of meditation which results in absorption into the Self where even the thought 'I am the Self' is not there."

"How can I absorb into the Self without 'I' doing it? Does it happen by itself, with no effort?"

"In the beginning after you put forth effort to let go off all thoughts, maintain only one thought 'I am the Self.' This requires effort, no doubt."

"Then?" Anveshak was curious.

Swamiji smiled and closed his eyes. Anveshak noticed indescribable peace on his face. "Even that thought will vanish in His overwhelming presence. He alone will remain, not 'I.' There will be no distinction for there will be nothing else apart from Him."

Anveshak thought back to the time when he had stood on the Golden Gate Bridge. He had been wrought with remorse, shame, dejection, and pain. Now he was preparing to take the leap with peace, freedom, and ultimate joy on his mind. A world of difference! He shook his head, amazed with the turn his life had taken.

He silently took leave of Swamiji, who sat in silence in front of Gurudev's large portrait in the meditation room.

A few days later, he picked up his ringing phone and saw on the caller ID that it was from the āśrama. When he answered, he heard Swamiji greeting him. In a few minutes, Swamiji explained why he was calling: Guruji Swami Tejomayananda was coming to Krishnalaya Āśrama in Piercy. Did Anveshak want to come and be part of the week-long camp there? Anveshak thought quickly. Of course! This was a wonderful opportunity that was not to be missed. He asked Swamiji if he could bring along some friends. Swamiji gave his consent and hung up after giving him some more details.

Anveshak recalled Gurudev's words about how the Supreme was like the thread holding the pearl necklace of all facets of the world together. He realized that Gurudev himself was the thread that connected him with the group of people who had helped him reverse the

*Guruji Swami Tejomayananda sings a bhajan at
Krishnalaya in Piercy, California.*

course of his life — Dr. Sevadas, Shantiji, the yoginī, the professor, and Swamiji. He felt the great compassion of the Master wash over him. After collecting himself, he called his friends and guides to tell them of the upcoming event. All agreed to clear their calendars and head to the camp at Krishnalaya.

The first day in Piercy turned out to be an unparalleled one for Anveshak.

Pūjya Guruji Swami Tejomayananda began by singing his composition "Gurudev tava mahanīya kṛpā," dedicated to Gurudev. Guruji's rendition moved Anveshak in ways he didn't know was possible. He felt an outpouring of love, gratitude, and reverence. He closed his eyes, not knowing that tears fell from them. Even as Guruji began his talk, Anveshak sat reveling in those feelings. His eyes flew open when he thought he saw the same image he had seen on the bridge, in what seemed like another lifetime. Gurudev!

When he was able to pull his thoughts together, he focused on what Guruji was saying, as he was quoting Gurudev:

In short, Vedānta points to a center in ourselves which is our own Truth, which is nowhere above the clouds. It is here, right here, just behind the mind. How do we discover it? Open your eyes and look. Remove the name, form, shape, properties, qualities, and relationships. What is perceived there? What is perceived in and through this purified, elevated mind is Brahman. It is meditation of the highest order. Reach it by any means you know. All are spiritual paths. Realize the Truth and then live to serve. Till then, you do not live. You merely exist. Try to wake up and live. Wake up!

Anveshak barely spoke after the talk. The next morning, he got up early and went to Gurudev's *kuṭiyā*, the place where Gurudev had stayed when he had delivered discourses on the entire *Bhagavad-gītā*. The silence in the inner room seemed to wrap itself around him. As if in a cocoon, Anveshak stood riveted looking at Gurudev's bed and other personal items used by Gurudev, placed neatly as if he were still living there. He quietly lowered himself to the ground in one corner of the room and closed his eyes.

'I am Brahman, the Self — the indescribable, ungraspable, formless, beyond the senses, eternal, omnipresent, all-pervading, most subtle, the womb of the entire creation ....' He recalled the words from Swamiji's guided meditation sessions.

His mind hardly wavered and he experienced utter stillness. All the same, he felt Gurudev's compassion washing over him and was overwhelmed with gratitude for the Grace he had been receiving.

After this intense experience, Anveshak barely felt the need to speak at all in the days that followed. His mind was quiet and there was little that bothered him. He went about doing sevā with equanimity and joy. His calm and positive attitude brought cheer around

Gurudev's kuṭiyā in Krishnalaya āśrama in Piercy, California

him. He recalled some words by Gurudev that had inspired him:

> The world has existence; the world is not existence. Just as you have health; you are not health.
>
> I am not the body; nor am I the body. The body is in me.
>
> Existence alone is my nature.
>
> Neither have I commission nor any omission. I am pure Consciousness.

Guruji having bhikṣā at Krishnalaya āśrama in Piercy, California

Every morning, Anveshak spent quiet moments in Gurudev's *kuṭiyā*, experiencing a stillness that remained in him through the day. He made no attempt to seek out others' company, until on the last day of the camp when Shantiji invited the group to join her in serving bhikṣā to Pūjya Guruji. After eating a sāttvika meal cooked with love by Shanti, and enjoying being in the compassionate presence of Guruji, all of them bid a loving and respectful farewell to Guruji, who was leaving Krishnalaya to continue with his U.S. tour. After cleaning up, the small group went out to the āśrama garden to enjoy the quiet evening. Swamiji, too, to their delight, joined them.

True to nature, it was Yoginī Damayanti who brought smiles on all their faces. Noticing Anveshak sitting with a straight back and cross-legged on the grass at the feet of Swamiji, she remarked, "The body sits still, the mind is in control!"

"The mind has been seduced by sevā!" added Dr. Sevadas.

"The heart is full, Anveshak sees the One in the many," Shanti said.

Anveshak looked around. Nature in the form of this garden, the temple courtyard, and the parks by the yoga studio were often the scene of his rebelliousness and learning, doubts and understanding. He wondered how he had not realized before that the shades of the trees, the perfume of the flowers, and the expansiveness of the skies — all were the hand of the Supreme guiding him to discover the divinity in it all.

"Now he finds the many in the One," said Professor Vidyadhar.

"When will I be with the One?" Anveshak whispered almost to himself.

Swamiji gently patted the head of Anveshak and quoted Gurudev:

> The supreme Ideal is the center within us, and we all exist on its circumference. Clicking in is a matter of adjustment to that center within. But clicking in seems to happen for some people and not for others, because some of us are standing on the circumference with our vision turned outward from it. All we have to do is turn around, face the center, and move on a radius to the center. … The only difference between those of us who are able to click in and those who are not is the capacity of the individual to turn around to the inner Self. That is all.

"Anveshak has turned inward, Swamiji," said Vidyadhar. Swamiji smiled.

Soon, all of them, aware that the next day was a working day, decided to pack up and head home. Anveshak decided to stay back for a day more to spend quiet hours in meditation in Gurudev's kuṭiyā.

So excited was he about being in Gurudev's kuṭiyā, he woke up at 2:30 A.M. the next morning. He just couldn't sleep anymore. He quickly took a cold shower and walked toward the kuṭiyā, enjoying the sight of the setting moon and the cool breeze blowing from the mountains. Anveshak slipped into the room and sat quietly. He felt an intense energy in the room. He could bring the mind to stillness even while keeping his eyes open. He looked toward the large window next to the bed. It was dark outside, and due to the dim light inside the room, his own reflection in the window glass looked back at him.

He withdrew his attention from the reflection and shifted to the glass, then slowly to his eyes, to the thought 'I am seeing,' to the 'I am'… moments later he felt a powerful presence within himself. It was as if an electric charge were passing through every nerve in his body. He couldn't pinpoint its source.

Was his mind deluding him?

Consciously but with ease, Anveshak abandoned that thought and again stilled his mind: 'I am Pure Existence.' An image floated in front of his eyes. What was that? He turned to see if it was the window drapes fluttering. No. He looked closer, straining to identify what he saw. He drew a blank. Maybe lack of sleep had blurred his sight? He closed his eyes and snapped them open quickly.

The apparition was still there. Anveshak gasped.

It was the same apparition from the Golden Gate Bridge! It was

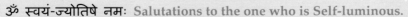

ॐ स्वयं-ज्योतिषे नमः Salutations to the one who is Self-luminous.

The Sun does not illumine the world. Light itself is the nature of the Sun, and in its presence everything gets illumined. Similarly, Consciousness is of the nature of Awareness, which is self-effulgent, and in Its presence, everything becomes known — illumined!

Light needs no introduction; so, too, is the self-effulgent Self.

Gurudev! Again! Yes, Yes! It was Gurudev smiling! There could be no mistake! He was sure!

Anveshak's wide-open eyes, opened even wider if it were possible. Even as he was grappling with what he was seeing, a deep voice thundered: "Tat Tvam Asi — You Are That." He could recognize it at once. It was He! Gurudev!

Anveshak stilled. He saw Gurudev looking intensely into his eyes. His mind went blank. There were no ripples of thoughts. He lost awareness of his body. He felt limbless and light as a feather. A complete and deep silence prevailed. In that silence, he felt himself afloat! He closed his eyes and yet he could still feel Gurudev's eyes looking at him. Was he dreaming? Anveshak barely breathed; he did not want anything to interfere with the moment. Then, once again, he heard the thundering voice clearly:

> YOU ARE NOT LOST IN YOUR DREAM! YOU WERE DREAMING
> YOU WERE LOST!

Anveshak's eyes were still closed. What dream was this? Then, like a bolt from the blue, came a new awareness: I am fully awake. I see myself disconnected from my body awareness. I am in the body as well as outside it. My mind feels light, free of burden. At will, I am able to bring it to stillness. Joy envelops me. I see the vast expanse of space, above, below, and everywhere. I feel illumined from within. I see a brilliant light emanating from my heart, and its effulgence

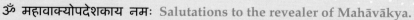

ॐ महावाक्योपदेशकाय नमः **Salutations to the revealer of Mahāvākya.**

The quintessence of Vedānta is contained in four Great Statements — great aphoristic declarations of the supreme Truth. They are direct revelations of Brahman. They are essentially for the seeker to contemplate and gradually discover the identity between his own essential Self and the supreme Reality.

From falsity to truth, darkness to light, and death to immortality is the spiritual journey; the great statements are the signposts!

penetrating into every cell in my body. I see that very light passing through everything in the room, connecting all into One!

All of a sudden, the vision of Gurudev dissolved. Anveshak opened his eyes and sat there staring into the space where it had been. It was a long time later that he stood up in the dimly lit room. He was almost bouncing with joy. He fell on the ground, prostrating with his entire body stretched out, at that very spot where he had seen Gurudev. He touched the carpet and he felt indescribable joy coming out of that touch. He felt the same joy enveloping his entire body. With an effervescence he had never felt before, he slowly stepped out of Gurudev's kuṭiyā. In the moonlight, he saw the Śivaliṅga next to the pathway. He reverentially touched it. A strange feeling of energized joy passed through him. He felt the same when he went closer to the plants, flowers, and trees. He experienced Life!

He felt alive! He quickly packed his bag, and as he drove out of the āśrama, the sun was breaking out and it seemed like a new dawn, a dawn never before experienced. Anveshak did not even realize that he had driven over four hours, until he reached the Golden Gate Bridge, a place he had not visited in a long, long time. It was like it had been on that fateful day: not golden, not a gate, and fighting to be seen through the fog.

He got out of his car and walked with a jaunt to the side of the bridge and peered down. The blue waters were beautiful. Then he looked up toward the sky, which was turning orange from the morning sun. Throwing his arms wide open, the wind whipping around him, he yelled in ecstasy: 'I' IS LOST!

Glossary

A	*Ādi Śaṅkarācārya*	one of Hinduism's greatest seers who propounded the Advaita Vedānta school of philosophy
	Ādi Śeṣa	the primordial snake; the thousand-headed serpent on which Lord Viṣṇu rests
	ahiṁsā	non-injury at the physical and mental level
	Ahura Mazda	the highest spirit of worship in Zoroastrianism, revolving around three basic tenets: good thoughts, good words, and good deeds
	Allah	Arabic word for God; used by Muslims to refer to God in Islam
	anantaśayana	the reclining pose of Lord Viṣṇu
	ārati (ārtī)	the concluding part of a pūjā, showing light in front of a deity, representing the burning of the ego
	asaṅgata	detachment; moving without obstacle
	āśrama	the residence and teaching center of a spiritual teacher, which often includes lodgings for his or her students; a stage of human life according Hindu scriptures
	Ātman	the essential divinity in each individual; the Self, pure Consciousness, the immanent aspect of the supreme Reality; this same Consciousness, when regarded as transcendent, is called Brahman.
	avidyā	ignorance of the Ātman as one's true nature; at the macrocosmic level, called Māyā
B	*Badrinath*	one of the four great Himalayan pilgrimage centers; established by Ādi Śaṅkarā in the 9th century.
	Bhagavad-gītā	"Song of God"; a major scriptural poem in eighteen chapters, contained in the *Mahābhārata*. In its 18 chapters, Lord Kṛṣṇa gives the divine Truth to his friend and

disciple Arjuna in the setting of a battlefield of the dynastic war between the Pandavas and Kauravas. It is a practical guide to persons attempting to live a spiritual life in their everyday living.

bhajan	a devotional hymn
bhajana	devoted service
bhakta	one who follows the path of devotion
bhakti	devotion; the path of devotion, one of the four main paths to liberation
bhāvana	an attitude or mood that one assumes toward the Divine
bhikṣā	a meal served to a monk, or renunciate
brahmacharya	one who practices spiritual discipline such as celibacy
Brahman	the indescribable, all-pervading, supreme Reality
D *Dakṣiṇāmūrthi*	an aspect of Lord Śiva as Guru of all types of knowledge
G *Gaṇeśa*	god of wisdom, invoked at the start of any new enterprise; worshiped as the remover of all obstacles; first son of Lord Śiva and his consort Goddess Pārvatī
guṇā	thought quality or texture; three in number: sattva, rajas, and tamas
guru	one who dispels darkness; a spiritual teacher who guides the seeker toward liberation
Gurudev tava mahanīya kṛpā — a composition in Hindi by Pūjya Guruji Swami Tejomayananda for Pūjya Gurudev
H *Hari Om*	greeting of another with reverence, mainly practiced among members of Chinmaya Mission
Holy Grail	sought-after Christian relic; believed to a be a cup that Jesus drank from at his Last Supper with his twelve disciples
I *Indiana Jones*	Hollywood film where the protagonist searches for the Holy Grail, finds it, and then loses it

	Īśvara	Consciousness functioning through Māyā as the God Principle
J	*japa*	repetition of a mantra to the exclusion of all other thoughts so as to build concentration of the mind
	japa māla	108 prayer beads strung together; used as an aid in meditation
	jīva	state of Ātman seemingly identified with the body, mind, and senses; the ego
	jīva bhāva	awareness of the body, mind, and senses
	jñāna mārga	the path of Knowledge; one of the four main paths to liberation
	jñānam	divine Knowledge
K	*Kargil*	territory on the Indian border which was defended bravely by Indian soldiers
	karma	the sum of the effects of past actions; action, work.
	kīrtanam	one of the nine modes of bhakti; singing
	kriyā	cleansing practice in hatha yoga
	Kṛṣṇa	an incarnation of Lord Viṣṇu, one whose teachings are found in the *Bhagavad-gītā*
	kuṭiyā / kuṭīra	cottage where swamis live
M	*mahātmā*	'Great Soul'; used to address one of great wisdom and, often, selflessness
	mananam	reflection on knowledge gained from the teacher and the scriptures to render that knowledge free from doubt
	mangalsūtra	necklace tied by the groom on his bride; worn by the wife as a sign of marital status
	mantra	a chosen name of God that a seeker repeats to himself to purify the mind
	Māyā	the concept of illusion; the root cause of non-apprehension of Reality; power of God
	Meera/Meerabai	a mystic renowned for her devotion to Lord Kṛṣṇa
	Mt. Kailash	in the Himalayas; considered among the most venerated of places on earth; earthly abode of Lord Śiva
	Muṇḍaka Upaniṣad	(also, *Muṇḍakopaniṣad*) a mantra Upaniṣad,

		i.e., having the form of a mantra part of the *Atharva Veda*
	mumukṣu	a seeker who has a burning desire for liberation
N	*naimittika karma*	occasional obligatory duties of the individual
	namaskāra	traditional Indian greeting done with folded hands
	Nārāyaṇa	an epithet for Lord Viṣṇu
	nitya karma	daily duties of the individual
P	*pādasevanam*	one of the nine modes of bhakti; serving at the feet of the lord
	parikramā	circumambulation of sacred places such as temples
	Parsi	practitioners of Zoroastrianism; those who fled persecution in Persia and now live in India
	Piercy	town near the Eel River in northern California; location of the Chinmaya Mission āśrama 'Krishnalaya'
	pradhan	primary; chief; president of a panchayat
	praṇāma	greeting of humility and reverence, usually by touching the feet of an elder or holy person
	prasāda	religious offering to the Lord, distributed to devotees after a pūjā
	pratishta	consecration of the temple idol
	prema	selfless love of God
	pūjā	worship, ritual
	pūjya	worshipful; reverential address to a holy person
R	*rajas (rājasika)*	one of three thought textures that typify the human personality; characterized by action, agitation.
	Rāma	the eighth incarnation of Lord Viṣṇu; hero of the epic *Rāmāyaṇa* written by Sage Vālmīki
S	*sādhanā*	spiritual practice which leads to one withdrawing the mind from worldly matters with the aim of attaining liberation

	sādhaka (sadhak)	seeker who follows specific sādhanās
	sādhya	goal of sādhanā
	samādhi	a trance-like experience of divine ecstasy; state of complete abidance in Pure Consciousness; a calm and pure mind in all circumstances
	satsaṇga	in the company of one's Guru; participating in an assembly of people all seeking the highest Truth
	sat-cit-ānanda	absolute existence-knowledge-bliss; an epithet for Brahman
	sattva (sāttvika)	one of three thought textures that typify the human personality; characterized by purity and serenity
	sevikā (sevak)	devotee, volunteer worker
	Śiva (Shiva)	God in the aspect of Dissolution, or Destroyer
	Śivaliṅga	a symbol of union of the duality of Śiva (Pure One) and Śakti (sacred force, empowerment, or cosmic energy)
	śodasa upacarā	sixteen-step worship of the Lord
	sneha	the first form of love in bhakti yoga; the heart softened by love
	śravaṇam	hearing of spiritual knowledge from a Guru; a prescribed spiritual practice
	Śrī Kṛṣṇa Śaraṇam Mama	an eight-syllable mantra; Lord Kṛṣṇa is my refuge
	Star Wars	Hollywood film with an intergalactic plot
T	*tamas (tāmasika)*	one of three thought textures that typify the human personality; characterized by dullness and inertia
	tat tvam asi	"That Thou Art"; a declaration of the supreme Truth from the *Chāndogya Upaniṣad*
	tulsī	holy basil plant
U	*Upaniṣads*	108 in all; the final, philosophical portion of the Vedas, the study of which is known as Vedānta
V	*Vaikuṇṭha*	the eternal abode of Lord Viṣṇu
	vairāgya	dispassion; indifference to worldly objects
	vāsanās	inborn dispositions and urges in the

	unconscious; impressions formed in the personality formed by actions driven by egocentric desires
Vedānta	teaches that the purpose of one's life is to realize the Supreme; evolved from the Upaniṣads; school of philosophy founded by Ādi Śaṅkarācārya
Vedas	four ancient scriptural texts, compiled by the poet-sage Vyasa from prophetic declarations handed down from teacher to the taught; they are the *Ṛg Veda, Yajur Veda, Atharva Veda,* and *Śama Veda.*
vijñānam	knowledge gained through experience
Viṣṇu	God in the aspect of Protector, or Preserver; one of the Hindu Trinity, the other two being Śiva and Brahma
Viṣṇu-sahasranāma-arcanā —	translated literally to "recitation of 1,000 names of Viṣṇu," one of the most sacred and commonly chanted stotras in Hinduism
viveka	discrimination between the unreal and the Real
viviktadeśa sevanam	retreating within; resorting to aloneness
Vyasa (Vyāsa)	the poet-seer who compiled the oral tradition of sacred teachings into written form, thus preserving the Vedas
Y *yātrī*	a pilgrim; a traveler
yoga	from the saṁskṛta root 'yuj,' "to join, to yoke"; the joining of the self to the supreme Self
yoginī	practitioner of yoga according to Saṁskṛta Sābdārthā Kaustubha

TRANSLITERATION AND PRONUNCIATION GUIDE

In the book, Devanāgarī characters are transliterated according to the scheme adopted by the International Congress of Orientalists at Athens in 1912. In it, one fixed pronunciation value is given to each letter; f, q, w, x and z are not called to use. An audio recording of this guide is available at www. chinmayamission.com/scriptures.php. According to this scheme:

	sounds like			*sounds like*
a	o in son		ḍh	dh in ad*h*esive
ā	a in *f*ather		ṇ	n in u*n*der*
i	i in *d*ifferent		t	t in *t*abla
ī	ee in *f*eel		th	th in *th*umb
u	u in *f*ull		d	th in *th*is
ū	oo in *b*oot		dh	dh in Gan*dh*i
ṛ	rh in *rh*ythm*		n	n in *n*ose
ṝ	**		p	p in *p*en
ḷ	**		ph	ph in *ph*antom*
e	a in ev*a*de		b	b in *b*oil
ai	i in del*i*ght		bh	bh in a*bh*or
o	o in c*o*re		m	m in *m*ind
au	o in n*o*w		y	y in *y*es
k	c in *c*alm		r	r in *r*ight
kh	kh in *kh*an		l	l in *l*ove
g	g in *g*ate		v	v in *v*ery
gh	gh in *gh*ost		ś	sh in *sh*ut
ṅ	an in *an*kle*		ṣ	s in *s*ugar
c	ch in *ch*uckle		s	s in *s*imple
ch	ch in wit*ch**		h	h in *h*appy
j	j in *j*ustice		ṁ	m in i*m*provise
jh	jh in *Jh*ansi		ḥ	**
ñ	ny in ba*ny*an		kṣ	tio in ac*tio*n
ṭ	t in *t*ank		tr	th in *th*ree*
ṭh	**		jñ	gn in *gn*osis
ḍ	d in *d*og		'	a silent 'a'

* These letters do not have an exact English equivalent. An approximation is given here.

** These sounds cannot be approximated in English words.

Patrons and Contributors

Grateful acknowledgement and special thanks are given to the following:

DAVID & MARGARET DUKES

| TORONTO, ONTARIO, CANADA |

All Chinmaya Mission Los Angeles families
who performed Guru Pādukā Pūjā
in the birth centenary year of our beloved
Pūjya Gurudev Swami Chinmayananda

|LOS ANGELES, CALIFORNIA, USA|